Find and Use Your Spiritual Gifts

Find and Use Your Spiritual Gifts

by

John E. Packo

Christian Publications, Inc.
Harrisburg, Pennsylvania

Christian Publications, Inc.
25 S. 10th Street, P.O. Box 3404
Harrisburg, PA 17105

The mark of ℭ𝒫 *vibrant faith*

Library of Congress Catalog Card Number: 80-69967
ISBN: 0-87509-293-4
Scripture quotations from the New American Standard Bible, © The
Lockman Foundation 1960, 1962, 1963, 1968, 1971, 1972, 1973, 1975, are
used by permission.
Quotations from THE NEW INTERNATIONAL VERSION, NEW
TESTAMENT © 1973 by the New York Bible Society International are
used by permission.
Printed in the United States of America

Contents

Preface   7

Part One

Understanding the Basics   9

1   What You Should Know about the Gifts   10
2   Spiritual Gifts Are for Ministry   19
3   Prepare Yourself to Recognize the Gifts   25

Part Two

Defining the Spiritual Gifts   31

4   Gifts of Prophecy, Helps, Teaching,
        and Exhortation   33
5   Gifts of Giving, Administration, Mercy, and
        Celibacy   41
6   Gifts of Word of Wisdom, Word of Knowledge,
        Faith, and Healings   48
7   Gifts of Miracles, Discernment, Tongues, and
        Interpretation of Tongues   56
8   Gifts of Apostleship, Evangelism, Shepherding,
        and Hospitality   64

Part Three

Testing to Determine Your Gifts   72

9   Test to Help Determine Your Gifts   74
10   Test to Help Confirm Your Gifts   82

Part Four

Developing and Using Your Gifts *91*

11 The Gifts Need to Be Developed *93*
12 The Gifts Need to Be Used *99*
13 The Church Needs to Function with Your Gifts *106*

Bibliography *115*

Preface

Several years ago the author visited a church whose pastor preached a sermon on "How You Can Know Your Spiritual Gifts." At the conclusion of the message he made it known that he along with his associate had set a goal to help each member discover his spiritual gifts. The possibilities of this approach made a deep impression and I thought about unlocking this potential in the congregation where I ministered. It would surely result in an enlarged ministry.

About this time a number of books became available on this subject and it was not difficult to find material. After careful research and preparation I preached a separate message on each gift. The series was a good introduction into the subject but did not go far enough to enable the believers to discover or use their gifts.

At this juncture it was obvious that there was a need for inter-action with individual believers on this subject. Material which provided a procedure for the use of pastors, elders, or teachers, in assisting believers to discover and use their spiritual gifts was the next objective. Some basic concepts, a position statement, and the specific characteristics of each gift should be included. A means of evaluation also seemed necessary along with the infor-mation on gift development and use.

With this basic outline of needs, research began in the avail-able resources in the field of spiritual gifts. The fruit of that research coupled with congregational experience resulted in this thirteen-lesson manual written with the adult Sunday school or training class in mind.

These lessons have been designed to help both student and teacher achieve the following goals:

1. To be knowledgeable in both the basic principles and characteristics of the spiritual gifts.

2. To have identified at least one of his spiritual gifts.

3. To be made aware of other believers' spiritual gifts and seek to complement them with his for effective ministry.

4. To experience joy through this interrelated ministry.

Unless otherwise indicated, Scripture quotations are from the *King James Version* of the Bible. Scripture quotations marked NASB are from the *New American Standard Bible* (copyright 1960, 1962, 1968, 1971, 1972 by the Lockman Foundation). Quotations marked NIV are from *The New Testament—New International Version* (copyright 1973 by the New York Bible Society International). Those marked Phillips are from *The New Testament in Modern English* (rev. ed. copyright 1958, 1960, 1972 by J. B. Phillips).

Grateful acknowledgement is expressed to Bobby Clinton for the use of basic ideas in his book, *Spiritual Gifts* in chapter 11, on "How to Develop Your Gift" and to Fuller Evangelistic Association for the use of the "Spiritual Gifts Profile," "Personal Interview Form" and "Job Description" sheet in chapter 12 which has been modified in this manual.

Part One

Understanding the Basics

The longest biblical passage dealing with the subject of spiritual gifts (1 Cor. 12-14) is introduced by these words:

> *Now about spiritual gifts, brothers, I do not want you to be ignorant* (1 Cor. 12:1, NIV).

The Corinthian believers were ignorant about the proper use of the gifts which were important in the life of the early Church. So the Apostle Paul instructed them in the basic understanding of the gifts to correct their misuse.

You can ask the average Christian the question, "What are your spiritual gifts?" Most of the time the answer will be, "I don't know." The tragedy today is that the average Christian is ignorant of the Bible teaching on gifts and that they lead to a joyful ministry. Unfortunately this has been true throughout church history until recently when interest in this subject has gained a wider popularity. Dr. Peter Wagner states that "more literature has been produced on the subject of spiritual gifts since World War II than in the previous 1,945 years put together."[1] The revival of interest in gifts in many instances has generated abuse and confusion.

The best antidote is sound teaching. It is imperative that we understand clearly the basic principles regarding gifts and their use as set forth in the Bible before we define, discover, and develop our spiritual gifts.

1

What You Should Know about the Gifts

Spiritual gifts are imparted by the Holy Spirit according to 1 Corinthians 12:1. The Greek word used for spiritual gifts in this verse is *pneumatikon* meaning literally, "spirituals" or "things of the Spirit." With the article, this word directs attention to the source, the Holy Spirit. However, the regular Greek word for spiritual gifts, *charisma*, is used five times in this chapter (1 Cor. 12:4, 9, 28, 30, 31). Thayer defines *charisma* as "a gift of grace; a favor which one receives without any merit of his own."[2] This forms the proper basis for understanding how the gift is given. The gift is unmerited by the believer. He does not have the right to it through any achievements. A spiritual gift is a special ability given by the Holy Spirit according to grace. It is interesting to note that the following terms are derived from the same root word:

chara	= joy
charis	= grace
charisma	= gift
charismata	= gifts

It can be concluded that joy results from the use of the gifts which came from grace bestowed by the Holy Spirit. Dr. A. B. Simpson presents this preceptive insight:

> It is the eleventh verse in which we are told that all these gifts "worketh that one and self-same Spirit." Literally this means all these gifts worketh the Spirit Himself. The man is but the instrument.[3]

Dr. Simpson goes on to warn about abusing the grace of God:

> Whenever we see the spirit of self-display, human

exaltation and adulation, the advertising of men and the disposition to glory in even the most honored servants of God, we may know that we are on forbidden ground, and in danger of sacrilegiously abusing the grace of God and worshipping the creature more than the creator.[4]

Gifts Are Given According to the Will of the Spirit

Not only is the Holy Spirit the source of the gifts, but He gives gifts to each person exactly as He determines. The remainder of verse 11 states, "dividing. . .severally as he will." Since this is true, no spiritual gift is earned through self-effort nor is it a sign of spirituality. To demand a gift which may not be according to the will of God is contrary to scriptural teaching and allows the enemy to substitute imitations. Satan can counterfeit the gifts. The magicians of Pharaoh's court performed miracles (Exod. 7:11, 22). Today various religions have worshippers that perform miraculous deeds, heal the sick, and speak in tongues.

We are warned in 1 Corinthians 12:3 about counterfeits which are contrary to the will of God:

> *Wherefore I give to you to understand, that no man speaking by the Spirit of God calleth Jesus accursed; and that no man can say that Jesus is the Lord, but by the Holy Spirit.*

The test is clear. Does the gift honor Jesus Christ as Lord? This confession is the sign that one is speaking by the Holy Spirit. Gifts given according to the will of God will exalt Jesus as the Lord. The ministry of the Holy Spirit always glorifies Jesus (John 16:13). So the first step to gift discovery is to submit to the will of God.

Gifts Are Given to Every Believer

All believers are given at least one spiritual gift. The following verses underscore this marvelous truth:

*But to each one is given the manifestation of the
Spirit for the common good* (1 Cor. 12:7, NASB).
*But one and the same Spirit works all these things,
distributing to each one individually just as he wills*
(1 Cor. 12:11, NASB).
*Unto every one of us is given grace according to the
measure of the gift of Christ* (Eph. 4:7).

Every believer without exception is given a spiritual gift.

The Bible not only stresses this universality of gifts but
accountability to God for the use of the gifts. This twofold
emphasis is explained by the Apostle Peter, 1 Peter 4:10, NASB:

*As each one has received a special gift, employ it in
serving one another, as good stewards of the
manifold grace of God.*

Christians are stewards of their gifts. A New Testament steward
had the responsibility to care for his master's goods. The master
expected the steward to deal responsibly with the resources by
nurturing and multiplying them.

The parable of the talents in Matthew 25:14-30 illustrates the
awesome responsibility of stewardship. Three stewards were
entrusted with three different amounts of money. The first two
doubled their amounts and when the day of accounting finally
came they were called "good and faithful servants." Faithful is
the key word to remember in the use of spiritual gifts. The
tragedy is that the third steward hid his money rather than
using it for an investment. For this unfaithfulness he was
judged a "wicked and slothful servant." It is serious to hide a gift
and fail to use it. It is the steward's obligation to discover and use
his gifts.

What Gifts Are Not

The gifts of the Spirit are not the Gift of the Spirit. The term,
Gift of the Spirit, is associated with God's offer of the Holy Spirit
Himself to the believer. On the Day of Pentecost the Gift of the

12

Spirit was poured out on the believers. While the Gift of the Holy Spirit is God's promise of the indwelling of the Holy Spirit, the gifts are the Spirit-enabling abilities given according to the sovereignty of God. Jesus spoke the following words in anticipation of the Gift of the Holy Spirit:

> *If ye then, being evil, know how to give good gifts unto your children; how much more shall your heavenly Father give the Holy Spirit to them that ask him?* (Luke 11:13).

Spiritual gifts are not talents. Some confusion persists between knowing whether a spiritual gift is a natural talent or not. The rationale in the gift books generally agrees about the following distinctions:

Talents	Gifts
Natural ability	Supernatural ability
Present from natural birth	Present from new birth
Used to communicate on a natural level	Used to edify the saints and for evangelism
Benefit whole creation	Largely limited to church although church benefits mankind

Since gifts are not talents, we must be careful not to use natural ability to accomplish spiritual ministry. For talents depend upon natural power whereas gifts depend on Spirit enablement. One good example would be teaching. Teaching as a natural talent will not build up the saints in the spiritual realm. However, when the teacher becomes a believer, the Spirit may add the spiritual dimension, thus, enabling the teacher to minister to the believer. Oswald J. Sanders made this following observation:

> Frequently, though not always, the gifts bestowed accord with natural talents and endowments, but

they always transcend them. Spiritual gifts pertain to the spiritual birth of Christians, not their natural birth. They are supernatural, but make use of and increase the natural abilities possessed.[5]

Leslie Flynn gives this view about the use of talents for spiritual ministry:

Talents and gifts are related. Literary, oratorical, artistic, musical, or linguistic talents may be avenues through which the Holy Spirit will use a person's gifts. But writing, speaking, or vocal abilities are talents, not gifts.[6]

Spiritual gifts are not fruit of the Spirit. The fruit of the Spirit is listed in Galatians 5:22, 23 as "love, joy, peace, longsuffering, gentleness, goodness, faith, meekness and temperance" (self-control). So love, according to biblical usage is not properly considered a gift.

The following distinction can be made between the fruit of the Spirit and the gifts of the Spirit:

Fruit of Spirit	Gifts of Spirit
What a believer is	What a believer does
Related to character	Related to service
Every believer may bear all the fruit	Only certain number of gifts generally possessed
Fruit is singular	Gifts are plural
Fruit is eternal	Gifts are temporary

How do spiritual fruit and spiritual gifts relate to each other? The great love chapter (1 Cor. 13) demonstrates that the gifts of the Spirit can never operate in the will of God apart from the fruit of the Spirit. This double emphasis in 1 Corinthians 13:2, 3 stresses this vital relationship. In verse 2 the futility of gifts operating apart from love regards the person as useless:

And though I have the gift of prophecy, and understand all mysteries, and all knowledge; and though I have all faith, so that I could remove mountains, and have not charity ₍love₎, I am nothing.

In verse 3 the futility of gifts operating apart from love regards the gift as unprofitable:

And though I bestow all my goods to feed the poor, and though I give my body to be burned, and have not charity ₍love₎, it profiteth me nothing.

A terrible price is paid when spiritual gifts are not accompanied by love as the Corinthian church discovered. With all of the exercise of their spiritual gifts they experienced nothing but carnality and divisions. There is a need to test the ministry of gifts by this penetrating question, "Is love the motive behind the use of spiritual gifts?"

The Gifts Are for Today

Gift theology has two diverse and well-entrenched positions. Unfortunately these two views are labeled, "Charismatic" or "anti-Charismatic." The strife between these two camps is well known by evangelicals.

The anti-Charismatics believe that some of the gifts are not for today. They claim that the gifts of apostleship, prophecy, miracles, healing, tongues, interpreting tongues, and discerning spirits are temporary gifts. Others believe that none of the spiritual gifts are for today. Their proof text is 1 Corinthians 13:10 which states, "But when that which is perfect is come, then that which is in part shall be done away." They interpret the word, "perfect" as referring to the Word of God. They insist that when the Bible was completed the gifts which they interpret as "that which is in part" ceased to function.

In contrast to this view, the Charismatics believe that all of the gifts are in operation today. They also believe that after you are converted you must experience the baptism in the Holy Spirit with the evidence of speaking in tongues.

F. B. Stanger makes this observation about the movement:

> However, many who speak of themselves as "charismatics" are primarily concerned about one gift only—the gift of tongues. These persons should be identified as "glossolalists." Glossolalia is the technical name for preoccupation with the particular gift of tongues-speaking.[7]

Many Christians believe that they have no choice but to side with either view, but they feel uncomfortable with either position. However, a believer has a third view to follow. This third view disagrees with view one on its interpretation of 1 Corinthians 13:10, but believes that all of the gifts are for today.

Dr. Eldon Woodcock sets forth the interpretation of the third view:

> Nevertheless, the view that the gifts of prophecy and speaking in tongues terminated during or shortly after the apostolic period is simply not taught in Scripture. The "perfect" refers to the Lord Jesus Christ's Second Coming and to the Eternal State that He will institute after the Millennium.[8]

Stanton Richardson answers the question "Are the gifts for today?" in the following manner:

> Are the gifts for today? is answered in the verse "Till we all come in the unity of the faith. . ." (Eph. 4:13). Dare anyone conclude that we have already reached a unity of the faith?[9]

Furthermore, the third view disagrees with the Charismatics for its unscriptural emphasis on tongues as the evidence of the baptism in the Holy Spirit. Those who hold the third view are charismatic in the New Testament sense of the word and not by today's label. The position of The Christian and Missionary

Alliance is an example of the third view. Since its beginning nearly a century ago Alliance leaders have responded to the various revivals of interest in spiritual gifts by issuing position statements, the first in 1907 and another in 1963. The 1963 statement concluded with these words:

> We believe the scriptural teaching to be that the gift of tongues is one of the gifts of the Spirit, and that it may be present in the normal Christian assembly as a sovereign bestowal of the Holy Spirit upon such as He wills. We do not believe that there is any scriptural evidence for the teaching that speaking in tongues is the sign of having been filled with the Holy Spirit, nor do we believe that it is the plan of God that all Christians should possess the gift of tongues. This gift is one of many gifts and is given to some for the benefit of all.
>
> The attitude toward the gift of tongues held by pastor and people should be "Seek not, forbid not." This we hold to be the part of wisdom for this hour.[10]

Notes

1.   Peter Wagner, *Your Spiritual Gifts Can Help Your Church Grow* (Glendale: Gospel Light/Regal Books, 1979), p. 27.

2.   Joseph H. Thayer, *Greek-English Lexicon of the New Testament* (New York: American Book Company, 1889), p. 667.

3.   A. B. Simpson, *The Holy Spirit*, vol. 2, (Harrisburg: Christian Publications, Inc.), p. 97.

4.   Ibid. (The same page as the preceding note.)

5.   Oswald J. Sanders, *The Holy Spirit and His Gifts* (Grand Rapids: Zondervan Publishing House, 1973), p. 112.

6.   Leslie B. Flynn, *19 Gifts of the Spirit* (Wheaton: Victor Books/Scripture Press, 1974), p. 22.

7.   F. B. Stanger, *The Gifts of the Spirit* (Harrisburg: Christian Publications, Inc., 1974), p. 21.

8.   Eldon Woodcock, "The Source and Purpose of The Gifts," *The Alliance Witness* (Oct. 18, 1978), p. 25.

9. Stanton W. Richardson, *Studies in Biblical Theology,* vol. 3, (St. Paul: St. Paul Bible College, 1969), p. 139.

10. Christian and Missionary Alliance, *Seek Not—Forbid Not* (Nyack: Christian and Missionary Alliance), leaflet.

2

Spiritual Gifts Are for Ministry

One must first understand the biblical concept of the local church to understand gift ministry. The human body is the principal metaphor used to reveal the nature of the Church in relationship to the spiritual gifts. Christ is described as the head of His body the Church. This is clearly presented in the following verses:

> *And He put all things in subjection under His feet,*
> *and gave Him as head over all things to the church,*
> *which is His body, the fulness of Him who fills all in*
> *all* (Eph. 1:22, 23, NASB).

Believers make up the body of Christ and are individual members of it. "Now ye are the body of Christ, and members in particular" (1 Cor. 12:27). The use of the term body indicates that the Church is more than an organization—it is an organism which consists of sharing life between the interrelated parts.

It is no accident that all the main gift lists (Rom. 12; 1 Cor. 12; Eph. 4) are presented in the context of the body of Christ. Let us look at the context of the Romans gift list, the Corinthians gift list, and the Ephesians gift list to discover the ministry of the gifts in relationship to the body.

What the Context of the Romans Gift List Tells Us about Ministry

The Romans gift list is found in chapter 12:6-8. In the context the word "body" is listed three times (vv. 1, 4, 5). The term body in verse 1 is the believer's body. The believer's body is vital to the ministry and must be dedicated to the Lord as an instrument in carrying out the will of God. It is unfortunate that so many believers can quote Romans 12:1, 2 without realizing that these verses lead into the Romans gift list. Many believers stop with the words, "that ye may prove what is that good, and acceptable, and perfect will of God" (v. 2), and never realize that verses 3—6 tell the four following truths to prepare us to do the will of God in the area of gift ministry:

1. Pride has no place in gift ministry: ". . .not to think of himself more highly than he ought to think. . ." (v. 3).

2. Rate your ability with sober judgment: ". . .but to think soberly. . ." (v. 3).

3. Recognize that God does not expect any more from us than He has given to us: ". . .according as God hath dealt to every man the measure of faith" (v. 3).

4. Understand that the purpose of spiritual gifts is to minister to the whole body. This fourth point is set forth by verses 4—6 where the analogy of the human body is given in verse 4 and applied in verse 5. Verse 4 tells us that the human body has many parts in one body and that all of these parts do not have the same use. The following application is presented in verse 5: (1) many believers make up the single body of Christ; (2) the believers are mutually dependent on one another; (3) the believers have different gifts given by grace. Dr. Woodcock stresses this basic function of gift ministry:

> The purpose of the spiritual gifts and their manifestations is to minister tó the communion of believers and to benefit the entire body of Christ. This is a crucial point. It is very significant that whenever the New Testament writers discuss the spiritual gifts they do not ever consider them only in relation to individuals. . . It is the gifts that enable the members to make their distinctive contributions toward the functioning of the body of Christ as a whole.[1]

What the Context of the Corinthians Gift List Tells about Ministry

The analogy of the body in 1 Corinthians 12:12-27 is sandwiched between the two gift lists (1 Cor. 12:8-10 and 1 Cor. 12:28-29) and forms the most detailed account of the Church as a living organism. Dr. Stoesz made this observation:

> The Church is represented as an organism rather than an organization in which members are mechanically joined to Christ or to others. An organism consists of parts vitally related so as to rely on one another for life and growth in a common whole.[2]

These are the principles taught in 1 Corinthians 12:12-27:

1. We are placed into the body by Spirit baptism. "For by one Spirit are we all baptized into one body. . ." (v. 13). This work of baptism assures the unity of the various members for all true believers are united to Christ in a living union in the body. This Spirit baptism takes place at our new birth as indicated by the past (aorist) tense of baptism and the words, "were we all" (NASB). Dr. H. L. Turner said the following:

> In First Corinthians 12 the Church is set before us as the Body of Christ. We are informed that this *Body* has many *members*. We are advised as to who these members are—the "*we*" of verse 13. The "we" are *all* who call upon the name of Jesus Christ as Lord. We are told *how* they become members of the Body of Christ: "For by one Spirit are we all baptized into one body."[3]

Having been placed in the body by the Spirit we are not unrelated units, but united in spiritual life and ministry of service.

2. The body consists of many parts each of which is vital to the whole (vv. 14-17).

It would be foolish for a believer to think that because his gift is not as valuable as someone else's gift, he does not belong to the body. It would be equally absurd for the foot to say, "Because I am not the hand, I am not of the body." Each member should be

21

content with his Spirit-given gifts. The believer should never consider his gift so unimportant as to make it unnecessary to the body.

Also it is as illogical to maintain that the ministry is limited to one gift as it is to believe that the whole body is an eye. Unfortunately many believers think the gift of pastoring is the only ministry of the local church. This is as unnatural as asking an eye to hear and walk and talk!

3. God has arranged the parts in the body just as He desired (v. 18). Peter Wagner states the following:

> This means that not only has God organized the Body on the model of an organism, but also that He has gone so far as to determine what the function of each of the members should be. Therefore, if you decide to organize your church around spiritual gifts, you are simply uncovering what God has already willed for your particular segment of Christ's Body.[4]

4. All the parts are needed including those that appear to be weaker (v. 21).

The eye cannot say to the hand, "I have no need for you." The hand in its place is as needful as the eye in its place. The passage does not make it clear about what parts are apparently the weak parts (v. 22) nor what it means to give greater honor to the less honorable parts. Perhaps it means that the less spectacular gifts, such as helps and mercy, are as needful as the spectacular gifts of miracles and healings.

5. The members have an equal care for each other rather than separate interests (v. 25).

All the members must be dependent on each other for their gift ministry. No member should be regarded as separate from others. They should have the same care for one another and feel an equal interest in the health, harmony, and growth of the whole body.

6. Every member is affected by the pain or well-being of its parts (v. 26).

As a pain in the foot affects the whole body, so each member is affected by the suffering member. Likewise, when one is honored all rejoice. Every member shares both the pain and the rejoicing of a fellow member. When this caring and sharing becomes natural as breathing, the local church fellowship is functioning as a healthy organism and will experience growth.

What the Context of the Ephesians Gift List Tells Us about Ministry

One of the most important passages on New Testament ministry is Ephesians 4:11-12. To grasp this picture of ministry, study the following chart:

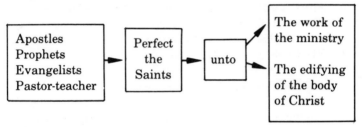

The clear teaching of Ephesians 4 is that every believer is to do the work of the ministry. It is important to realize how spiritual gifts relate to ministry. Remember that the Holy Spirit has gifted every believer (1 Cor. 12:11), and that God has determined what the function of your gift should be in the body (1 Cor. 12:18). Ministry is to be performed through your spiritual gifts. You may be thinking, "I can see now from this study that I'm to minister through my spiritual gift, but what is my spiritual gift and who is going to instruct me on how to use it?" The answers to those questions are found in this passage. The Lord Jesus has provided gifted leaders "to prepare God's people for works of service" (Eph. 4:11, NIV). So the pastor as the leader of the local church, along with the elders, is responsible for preparing the believers for ministry through their spiritual gifts. Keith Bailey relates this responsibility of leadership in the following manner:

Leadership at any level which does not seek to find

23

the gifts of the Spirit in the family of believers and cultivate the use of those gifts does not really understand its role. Christ has given every believer a gift for ministry to the whole body. The believer who has never learned to serve Christ and his brethren by exercising his gift is not yet mature. The preaching, teaching, shepherding, and oversight of official leadership should encourage every believer to be a functioning member of the body of Christ.[5]

The believer is not only prepared by the pastor-teacher for the work of ministry but also for the upbuilding of the body. When the spiritual gifts operate according to Ephesians 4:11-13, the body edifies itself and goes on to maturity.

Stanton Richardson said the following about the building up of the body:

> The building of the body seems to indicate the growth of the body. Their members passing from immaturity to maturity. Paul made reference to this in 1 Corinthians 13 that when he became a man he put away childish things, indicating that growth in truth leads out of childhood and into manhood.[6]

Notes

1. Woodcock, "Purpose of the Gifts," p. 26.
2. Samuel Stoesz, *Understanding My Church* (Harrisburg: Christian Publications, Inc., 1968), p. 41.
3. Harry L. Turner, *The Voice of the Spirit* (Harrisburg: Christian Publications, Inc., est. 1886), pp. 111, 112.
4. Wagner, *Your Spiritual Gifts,* p. 39.
5. Keith Bailey, *Servants In Charge* (Harrisburg: Christian Publications, Inc., 1979), p. 14.
6. Richardson, *Biblical Theology,* p. 126.

3

Prepare Yourself to Recognize the Gifts

As one reads the many books concerning gifts it soon becomes apparent that there are differences of opinion concerning the number of gifts and the classifications under which they are categorized. One of the reasons for this diversity is that a systematic classification of gifts is not found in the New Testament. Since this is true, in this study the gifts are listed in the order in which they appear in the New Testament and do not follow a systematic classification.

None of the four primary gift lists are complete in themselves. Many believe that even after you combine the gift lists they are not complete. Since there are gifts mentioned in verses other than the four gift lists, Peter Wagner believes in what he calls, "an open-ended approach" to the gifts.[1] Taking this open-ended approach he said, "The Bible does not lock us into tight restrictions as to the number of gifts."[2] Wagner has twenty-seven gifts in his gift list which includes voluntary poverty, martyrdom, missionary, intercession, exorcism, and recognizes that others might add the gift of music and craftmanship, increasing the number of the gift list.

Dr. Woodcock makes this observation:

> Even a contemplation of all the gifts mentioned throughout the New Testament would probably not be an exhaustive list of spiritual gifts. But the lists illustrate the kinds of things that the Holy Spirit accomplishes through believers.[3]

This problem of not knowing what gifts to include in a list arises from three areas of difficulty: (1) the spiritual gifts are not clearly defined; (2) any definitions of the gifts require interpretation; (3) some of the gifts have little more than word studies that can be used to identify them. (We cannot be dogmatic when this is the case.) Bobby Clinton correctly observed the following:

> Disagreements usually indicate the lack of conclusive biblical evidence upon which to resolve the question. Hence, be tolerant and allow others their views without dogmatically insisting upon your view.[4]

Another area of difficulty is that some gifts overlap. Prophecy incorporates some teaching as well as evangelism in some cases. The gift of helps and mercy are related. Donald Bridge addressed this dilemma when he said:

> It is a problem to know what New Testament writers meant by the different charisma. Several of the gifts appear to overlap as the difference between giving of aid and doing acts of mercy. Does a prophet also exercise wisdom or knowledge? While some gifts are clear-cut, some do not fit into neat categories, so this must be kept in mind for those who seek what God has done for them.[5]

In the following overview of gifts they are listed in the order in which they appear in the New Testament.

Romans 12:6-8—

prophecy	giving
helps	leadership
teaching	mercy
exhortation	

1 Corinthians 7:7—

celibacy

1 Corinthians 12:8-10, 28 adds—

wisdom	tongues
knowledge	interpretation
faith	apostle
healings	miracles
discerning of spirits	

Ephesians 4:11 adds—

evangelist   pastor

1 Peter 4:9 adds—

hospitality

Variety and Degree within Gifts

Since gifts are for ministry they must be exercised. The gift itself is not a ministry but the gift in use constitutes a ministry. The gifts are Spirit-given abilities for service to Christ and His Church.

In preparing yourself to recognize the gifts it is essential to realize that there are varieties of uses within each gift. A gift may be used for a great many different ministries. The gift of teaching may be used by one believer to teach in seminary, by another to teach children, while another may teach the teen Sunday school class.

Some believers have combinations of gifts. Some writers refer to a combination of gifts in one believer as a "gift mix." The discovery of a certain combination of gifts will enable a believer to minister in unusual service. An elder with a gift mix of teaching, wisdom, and healing could have a very effective ministry in the local church.

Not only is there a variety of uses for some gifts and gift mixes in some believers, but there are also degrees in the scope of ministry. One believer with the gift of evangelist may minister in the area of personal evangelism with converts numbering

27

several hundred over a lifetime of ministry. Another believer may minister in the area of public evangelism, such as Dr. Billy Graham, with huge crowds and have tens of thousands of converts in his lifetime.

Recognize That Duties Are Different from Gifts

Another area that could present misunderstandings is the confusion of gifts with "Christian duties." Just because a believer does not have the gift of mercy does not mean that he has no obligation to display mercy. If you do not have the gift of giving, that should not be an excuse for failing to contribute finances to the needs of the local church or some other charitable endeavor. When the Bible states, "Distribute to the necessity of the saints" (Rom. 12:13), it is not speaking exclusively to the saints with the gift of giving, but to all the saints. Though we do not all have the gift of discernment, yet all of us are to "Prove all things" (I Thess. 5:21). Though not all have the gift of evangelism, yet every believer is to be a witness.

The question is raised whether some gifts are restricted to men and not for use by women. Flynn gave the following reasoning that answers this question:

> No gift is restricted to either sex. All gifts are for both men and women. Even in groups which forbid women pastors, some women need the gift of pastoring in order to shepherd other women and children who might need their care. Women also require the gift of teaching to instruct other women and children. The gift of government is essential for those in places of leadership in women's groups.[6]

Steps to Gift Recognition

There are certain spiritual steps that must be taken by those who desire to discover their gifts. If any one of these is missing, difficulty will be experienced when trying to recognize your spiritual gift.

Here are the qualifications which are essential:

1. You must be born again.

Without it no one can possess a spiritual gift. The subsequent steps will not be valid if one has not been born again. One of the many benefits of salvation is receiving spiritual gifts.

> *But to each one of us grace was given according to the measure of Christ's gift. Therefore it says, "When he ascended on high, he led captive a host of captives, and he gave gifts to men"* (Eph. 4:7, 8, NASB).

Seek to find Christ as your personal Savior first before you seek to discover any spiritual gifts.

2. You must study very carefully what the Bible says about spiritual gifts.

It is difficult to accurately assess your gifts, if you have not studied the biblical meaning of the gifts. Do not try to take any shortcuts (2 Tim. 2:15).

3. You must confess any known sin in your life to Christ (1 John 1:9).

It is interesting that the subject of the gifts in Romans 12 is not introduced until salvation and sanctification have been explained in the first eleven chapters of the Book of Romans.

4. You must pray for wisdom throughout the process of gift discovery.

> *But if any of you lacks wisdom, let him ask of God, who gives to all men generously and without reproach, and it will be given to him* (James 1:5, NASB).

Notes

1. Wagner, *Your Spiritual Gifts*, p. 73.
2. Ibid., p. 57.
3. Woodcock, "Purpose of the Gifts," p. 26.

4.   Bobby Clinton, *Spiritual Gifts* (Coral Gables: West Indies Mission, 1975), p. 51.

5.   D. Bridge and D. Phypers, *Spiritual Gifts and the Church* (Downers Grove: InterVarsity Press, 1973), p. 12.

6.   Flynn, *19 Gifts,* p. 33.

Part Two

Defining the Spiritual Gifts

In this section each gift is considered in such a manner as to help you discover your particular gifts.

A working definition is given for each spiritual gift, followed by background information based on word studies along with some brief observations. Where possible, characteristics have been compiled from Bible examples of the gift in action. These characteristics are considered in their relationship to the motivation and manifestation of the gift. These are important keys to gift discovery.

Motivation is the Spirit-inspired desire to minister in love with a specific spiritual gift. Manifestation is defined as the experience that results from the Spirit-empowered use of your spiritual gift in ministry. Thus the spiritually gifted believer is motivated to accomplish a Spirit-empowered manifestation. The areas of motivation and manifestation are disclosed with each spiritual gift. They give a composite picture which is a valuable aid to gift discovery.

Divide the class into Discovery Groups of three persons each. Below is an evaluation chart which should be filled in by each person in a Discovery Group. You will notice three columns under the words, "Yes," "Maybe," "Not Sure," and "No." The first column is for self-evaluation; the second column is to evaluate the second person in your group; and the third column is to evaluate the third person in your group. After comparing notes with your group, place your conclusion of "Yes," "Maybe," "Not Sure," or "No" in the confirmation column.

The Discovery Groups should only fill out on the evaluation chart those gifts being considered in the lesson. The chart will be completed with the study of chapter 8.

Evaluation Chart

	Yes			Maybe			Not Sure			No			Confirm		
	1	2	3	1	2	3	1	2	3	1	2	3	1	2	3
1. Prophecy							√								
2. Helps										√					
3. Teaching							√								
4. Exhortation										√					
5. Giving				√											
6. Administration				√											
7. Mercy				√											
8. Celibacy	√														
9. Wisdom										√					
10. Knowledge										√					
11. Faith					√										
12. Healings										√					
13. Miracles										√					
14. Discernment								√							
15. Tongues										√					
16. Interpretation										√					
17. Apostleship										√					
18. Evangelism				√											
19. Shepherding							√								
20. Hospitality				√											

4

Gifts of Prophecy, Helps, Teaching, and Exhortation

The Gift of Prophecy

The gift of prophecy is the Spirit-given ability to receive and communicate timely Spirit-inspired messages from God's Word that result in edification, exhortation, and consolation (Rom. 12:6; 1 Cor. 14:3).

The word prophet comes from the Greek word, *prophetes,* which literally means, "forth-tell." A prophet tells forth God's messages which may involve foretelling (Acts 11:27-30). Prophets were God's spokesmen in the Old Testament who spoke to men on behalf of God (1 Pet. 2:21). Kittel states, "By and large the New Testament understands by the prophet the biblical proclaimer of the divine, inspired message."[1] Bridge and Phypers give the following insight:

> Most scholars agree that Old Testament prophets proclaimed God's Word to people and secondarily often predicted future events. The same combination of proclamation and prediction are found in the New Testament... This can be said to be at the heart of all Christian teaching. The Christian is commanded to live like Christ and to proclaim Him to others in the light of His predicted return when this present evil world will be destroyed.[2]

Both the Old and New Testament prophets had basic similarities. They received their messages from God and proclaimed the Word of God to the people. They denounced sin and warned against future judgment. They took a stand on national issues. They preached a message of repentance and predicted future events.

Prophecy directed to the believer brings three responses

according to 1 Corinthians 14:3. (1) It produces the upbuilding of Christian life and character; (2) encourages the discouraged believers and (3) strengthens the believers with hope.

An example of the gift of prophecy was John the Baptist who had the following characteristics according to Luke 3:3-20:
1. He was a bold and dynamic preacher (vv. 3, 7, 13, 14).
2. He was able to discern the motives of the people (v. 7).
3. He was direct and frank in speaking (vv. 7-14).
4. He preached for a decision (repentance) (v. 8).
5. He had the ability to identify evil (vv. 10-14).
6. He had the courage to openly reprove evil (v. 19).
7. The listeners' wills responded to the message (vv. 10, 12, 14).
8. He prophesied the Day of Pentecost (v. 16).

Motivations That Characterize the Gift of Prophecy

1. To preach openly against sin.
2. To correct the wrongs of society.
3. To take a strong stand on contemporary issues.
4. To wake up an indifferent church.
5. To preach messages on future judgment along with the return of Christ.

Manifestations That Characterize the Gift of Prophecy

1. Give timely messages that meet the needs of people.
2. Able to correct persons who have made mistakes.
3. Speak with such emotion that people are often moved to tears.
4. Speak with authority when God gives a message.
5. Believers receive edification, encouragement, and consolation from the message.

The Gift of Helps

The gift of helps is the Spirit-given ability to give practical assistance that will encourage other believers to fulfill their responsibilities (Rom. 12:7; 1 Cor. 12:28).

The gift appears in the Romans and Corinthians gift lists under two different Greek words which are *diakonia* (Rom. 12:7) and *antilempsis* (1 Cor. 12:28). However, both words have the same meaning of "Any discharge of service given in genuine love."[3] So the word properly denotes giving aid, assistance or lending a hand with the view of freeing others for spiritual ministries. By choosing the seven men to oversee the welfare distribution the apostles were able to devote more time to the ministry of prayer and the Word (Acts 6:2-4). The deacons had a supportive role that released the apostles to fulfill their responsibilities which resulted in an increase in the Word of God and a multiplication of disciples in Jerusalem (Acts 6:7).

Mark was another example of the helper. He ministered to Paul and Barnabas (Acts 12:25). Epaphroditus also assisted Paul by ministering to his needs (Phil. 2:25). In the Old Testament, Bezalel was filled with the Holy Spirit to assist with the construction of the tabernacle. Today believers with the gift of helps are needed to labor faithfully in church construction and maintaining present church buildings to keep them useful and attractive in appearance. Believers are needed who enjoy serving in the nursery, operating the mimeograph machine, producing the church bulletin, ushering, decorating for missionary convention, and a host of other ministries.

Martha is singled out as a person with the gift of helps. Her characteristics are recorded by Luke 10:38-42:

1. Martha had a tendency to do things herself.
2. She was not very articulate when she said bluntly, "Tell her to help me" (v. 40).
3. Servers may get negative when working with others.
4. She became absorbed with all the preparations being made.
5. Servers find it hard to say no, since they want to please others.
6. Martha saw the specific task rather than long-range goals.

Motivations That Characterize the Gift of Helps

1. To do little jobs which will free leadership to use their gifts.
2. To do work myself rather than enlisting aid from others.

3. To help people with short-term assignments.
4. To be quiet rather than outspoken.
5. To work with hands rather than speak before a group.

Manifestations That Characterize the Gift of Helps

1. Would rather assist a leader than be a leader.
2. Enjoy doing manual and menial jobs around the church.
3. Generally are the first to volunteer for manual jobs at the church.
4. Do not find it difficult to help others.
5. Satisfied to be a teacher's aid in a Sunday school class.

The Gift of Teaching

The gift of teaching is the Spirit-given ability to explain God's Word clearly so that believers may learn and apply it to mature their lives.

The gift of teaching is so important that it is found in the three major gift lists (Rom. 12:7; 1 Cor. 12:28; Eph. 4:11) and is listed third in the biblical order (1 Cor. 12:28). Teaching is a foundational gift. The apostles who had this gift (Acts 2:41, 42) began immediately after the three thousand were saved on the Day of Pentecost to give them instruction. The importance of teaching was reflected by Jesus who regarded Himself as a teacher (John 13:13). Jesus loved people and tried to teach them of spiritual realities (John 14:10). He taught not only by words but by example of His life which was a continual object lesson. His teaching emphasis was geared to making disciples. Jesus used the Scriptures to teach about Himself (Luke 24:27).

Stanley R. Allaby notes several main differences between secular and Christian educators. Here are two differences:

1. The Scriptures put a much greater emphasis on the personal example of the teacher than do secular education. . .for the most part the teacher's example was neglected in secular education. 2. The Scriptures put a much greater emphasis on making

36

disciples. Secular education is much more concerned with the transmitting of factual data.[4]

In the great commission (Matt. 28:18-20), the command to "make disciples" would be impossible apart from teaching. New believers need to be taught "to observe all that I commanded you."

Apollos was an example of the gift of teaching for he had the following characteristics (Acts 18:24-28):
1. He was able to express himself clearly (v. 24).
2. He had a good knowledge of the Scriptures (v. 24).
3. He taught with diligence and accuracy (v. 25).
4. He had a logical and analytical mind (v. 28).
5. He was a man of conviction (vv. 25, 26, 28).
6. His teaching was Christ-centered (v. 28).

Persons who possess this gift are patient with their students. They enjoy spending time preparing the lesson. They try to line up visual aids to get across a lesson. They explain material in a clear and understandable manner. The teacher expects his student to learn and grow in Christlikeness.

Motivations That Characterize the Gift of Teaching

1. To analyze Bible knowledge.
2. To systematize Bible knowledge.
3. To research in order to prove Bible truths.
4. To teach by truth and example so others will learn.
5. To instruct others in discipleship and Christlikeness.

Manifestations That Characterize the Gift of Teaching

1. Teaching in Sunday school has changed lives.
2. Explain truth in a clear manner so that people can understand it.
3. Usually research more material than can be used in one class period.
4. Spend time in word studies to assure accuracy.
5. The teaching ministry results in learning.

The Gift of Exhortation

The gift of exhortation is the Spirit-given ability to encourage and counsel a believer in his faith that the believer will experience comfort and guidance (Rom. 12:8).

The word used for exhortation in its noun form is *paraclete* which means, "One who is called alongside to comfort and counsel." The use of this word occurs in John 14:16 where Jesus sought to relieve the disciples' fear of His departure. He encouraged them by teaching that the Father would be sending "another Counselor" (NIV). This double meaning of comfort and counsel appears throughout Scripture. Kenneth Gangel presents this helpful insight:

> A good father is regularly engaged in both aspects of exhortation, sometimes in connection with the same incident within a few minutes of time. Paul even uses the paternal image as an example of exhortation in the leadership role of the church (1 Thess. 2:11).[5]

The believer with the gift of exhortation solves problems from the Word of God and relies upon the Holy Spirit to bring about all behavioral changes. The gifted believer confronts a troubled believer with the Word of God and with the aid of the Holy Spirit ministers to his need. God blesses this ministry of counseling within the body by bringing comfort and guidance to the disheartened believer and joy of service to the gifted believer. The pastor who discovers believers who have this gift will find it of tremendous help in the area of counseling. Generally elders with this gift would be a tremendous asset.

Barnabas illustrates a believer who possessed the gift of exhortation. The apostles called Joseph, a Levite from Cyprus, "Barnabas (which is, being interpreted, The son of consolation,)" (Acts 4:36). Here is his record:

1.   He counseled the disciples, who feared Paul, to accept him (Acts 9:26-28). They needed his help to dispel their fears and replace their fears with comfort.

2. He encouraged believers at Antioch to remain true to the Lord (Acts 11:19-24). Evidently Barnabas was successful for the believers made such an impression on the pagans that they were called "Christians," literally meaning, "little Christs."

3. His message gave encouragement and guidance to the believers (Acts 14:22).

4. He was positive and never gave up on people (Acts 15:39). After a sharp disagreement with Paul over Mark, Barnabas took Mark with him.

Motivations That Characterize the Gift of Exhortation

1. To encourage believers who are discouraged.
2. To go out of the way to cheer people.
3. To share Scriptures that will encourage others.
4. To counsel believers with the Word.
5. To search and find Scripture that will help persons solve problems.

Manifestations That Characterize the Gift of Exhortation

1. A person to whom people readily confide their problems.
2. Advise people as to the right course of action.
3. Demonstrate a good grasp of the subtilities of human nature.
4. Able to guide people through the difficulties that produce maturity.
5. Give helpful insights to those going through hurts as well as joys.

Notes

1. Gerhard Kittel, *Theological Dictionary of the New Testament* (Grand Rapids: Wm. B. Eerdmans Publishing Co., 1972), 6:828.
2. Bridge and Phypers, *Spiritual Gifts*, p. 40.
3. Kittel, *Theological Dictionary*, 2:87.

4. Stanley Allaby, "How to Discover and Test Whether You Have Teaching Gift," *The Journal of Pastoral Practice,* vol. 2, no. 2. (Phillipsburg: Presbyterian & Reformed Publishing, 1978), p. 176.
5. Kenneth Gangel, *You and Your Spiritual Gifts* (Chicago: Moody Press, 1975), p. 28.

5

Gifts of Giving, Administration, Mercy, and Celibacy

The Gift of Giving

The gift of giving is the Spirit-given ability to share generously and cheerfully money to further the work of God (Rom. 12:8).

While all Christians are expected to give, there are some with a special gift of giving. The word "simplicity" used in the King James Version is the clue to discovering this gift. Simplicity denotes giving that is liberal and without any personal end in view (2 Cor. 8:2; 9:11, 13; 11:3).

Kenneth O. Gangel defines cheerfulness in relationship to the gift:

> How many Christians give to God's work with "joyful eagerness"? Such an attitude is obviously significantly different from "devoted duty" or even "loyalty to the church."[1]

The Corinthians were instructed to give, "not grudgingly, or of necessity for God loveth a cheerful giver" (2 Cor. 9:7). The believer with the gift of giving gives cheerfully and freely because the Holy Spirit has imparted the love to give generously. He gives not for public attention (Matt. 6:3) but from love for God. He acquires his money through labor "performing with his own hands what is good, in order that he may have something to share with him who has need" (Eph. 4:28, NASB).

Barnabas exercised the gift of giving by selling his land and bringing the proceeds to the apostles (Acts 4:34-37). The believer with the gift of giving is not always a person of material wealth as testified by the widow who had the unselfish spirit of giving (Mark 12:42, 43). The study of Abraham, with the view of looking at his gift of giving, is an interesting one:

1. God entrusted him with material assets (Gen. 13:2; 24:1).
2. He had a reputation for his generous spirit (vv. 9-10).
3. He tithed without any pressure to do so (v. 20).
4. He was willing to share what was rightfully his with others (vv. 23, 24).
5. He was willing to sacrifice all if God required it (vv. 1-3).

Motivations That Characterize the Gift of Giving

1. To help others with money.
2. To make money primarily to give to the spread of the gospel.
3. To sacrifice all material good if God required it.
4. To share one's goods with the poor.
5. To encourage others to give sacrificially.

Manifestations That Characterize the Gift of Giving

1. Do without in order to give more to further the gospel.
2. Donate funds when confronted with urgent financial needs.
3. Regularly give more than 30 percent of personal income to the Lord's work.
4. Show the ability to handle material resources wisely.
5. Can readily recognize the material needs of others.

The Gift of Administration

The gift of administration is the Spirit-given ability to humbly lead others by example, and guide the members of the body to attain goals that glorify God (Rom. 12:8; 1 Cor. 12:28).

Two words are used in the gift lists to describe the gift of administration. Lead (Rom. 12:8, NASB) comes from the Greek word *prophistemi* which means "to stand before" and stresses "to care for" while leading. The Holy Spirit places some "to stand before" others in the church. This word is used to describe a father's rule over his family (1 Tim. 3:5, 12), and to the leader's care over the church (1 Thess. 5:12, 13; 1 Tim. 5:17).

The second word is found in the Corinthians gift list (1 Cor.

12:28). The Greek word, *kuberneseis* means "guiding to reach the goal." The term originated from the language of the sea and comes from a verb form that means "to steer a ship." Kittel states, "The importance of the helmsman increases in a time of storm."[2]

Romans 12:8 states "to lead with diligence." Diligence means "with haste or speed." How can a leader serve with speed? Peter Wagner gives this interesting insight:

> By maintaining his focus on the goal(s) to be achieved, monitoring the progress toward those goals and preventing the people from being side tracked in the pursuit of these goals.[3]

Nehemiah was an example of "leading with speed" which produced the following characteristics:
1. He had a special dedication for the cause of God's people (Neh. 1:4).
2. He had a sense of timing (Neh. 2:6).
3. He could sense the problems and survey the needs (Neh. 2:12-15).
4. He knew how to involve others in the work (Neh. 2:16-18).
5. He could organize both human and material resources (Neh. 3).
6. He could proceed under pressure and opposition (Neh. 4:6).
7. He knew how to delegate authority (Neh. 7:1, 2).

Jesus taught a unique kind of leadership in the local church which may be called a "servant leader." He set the contrast between the secular and servant leader in Matthew 20:25-28 (NIV):

> *Jesus called them together and said, "You know that the rulers of the Gentiles lord it over them, and their high officials exercise authority over them. Not so with you. Instead, whoever wants to become great among you must be your servant, and whoever wants to be first must be your slave—just as the Son of Man*

did not come to be served, but to serve, and to give his life as a ransom for many."

Motivations That Characterize the Gift of Leadership

1. To assume responsibility where leadership is absent.
2. To organize and motivate believers to do the Lord's work.
3. To provide leadership to enable believers to reach goals.
4. To lead a project to get work done with speed and effectiveness.
5. To serve the Lord by leading others.

Manifestations That Characterize the Gift of Leadership

1. Can organize people and programs to accomplish goals.
2. Feel comfortable serving in a position of leadership.
3. Find it easy to make decisions and give directives.
4. Endure pressure until a goal is accomplished.
5. Are willing and able to delegate authority.

The Gift of Mercy

The gift of mercy is the Spirit-given ability to work compassionately and cheerfully with neglected people (Rom. 12:8).

Believers having this gift minister to neglected saints in the body, but extend their ministry to the deprived, the outcast, the handicapped, the elderly, the retarded, the drug addict, and the underprivileged whoever they may be. Mercy means to pity, to have compassion, and to show gracious favor. The gift of mercy has the three basic ingredients of feeling pity, displaying cheerfulness, and acting to relieve the need. It springs from divine love that acts in Christ's name with the object of glorifying God. Whenever Jesus was moved with compassion He acted to heal the blind (Matt. 20:30-34), the lepers (Luke 17:11-14), and the sick (Matt. 8:16, 17). His whole life on earth demonstrated compassion.

The good Samaritan had all the characteristics of a believer with the gift of mercy (Luke 10:29-37):

1. He saw the stranger and was moved with compassion (v. 33).
2. He was drawn to the stranger who was hurt (v. 34).
3. He acted by binding up the man's wounds (v. 34).
4. He was sensitive to the embarrassment of the stranger who would not be able to pay, so he paid the bill (v. 35).
5. He had the ability to discern the inn keeper's sincerity in continuing the proper care (v. 35).

Motivations That Characterize the Gift of Mercy

1. To alleviate the suffering of humanity.
2. To remove emotional and physical pain from people.
3. To visit the lonely and shut-ins.
4. To minister to hopeless cases of humanity.
5. To be kind and loving to the unwanted.

Manifestations That Characterize the Gift of Mercy

1. Enjoy helping people who have physical or mental problems.
2. Talk cheerfully to those who are lonely or shut-ins.
3. Discover that your visitation ministry cheers the suffering.
4. Attracted to people who are in distress.
5. Take food baskets to feed the poor.

The Gift of Celibacy

The gift of celibacy is the Spirit-given ability to remain single without frustration (1 Cor. 7:7).

Paul classifies the state of celibacy as a spiritual gift (charisma). He related to the Corinthians that every man has his proper gift from God.

Likewise Jesus said in response to the disciples' answer not to marry, that "Not everyone can accept this teaching, but only those to whom it has been given" (Matt. 19:11-12, NIV). The term eunuch is employed figuratively by Jesus with reference to the power, given as a gift of grace, to have an indifference toward sexual desires. Peter Wagner gives this simple test to discover if you are celibate:

> If you are single and know down in your heart that you would get married in an instant if a reasonable opportunity presented itself, you probably don't have the gift. If you are single and find yourself terribly frustrated by unfulfilled sexual impulses, you probably don't have the gift. But if neither of these things seem to bother you, rejoice—you may have found one of your spiritual gifts.[4]

There are advantages to remaining single. Unmarried believers are more free to devote their time to the Lord's work than the married. Paul said, "One who is unmarried is concerned about the things of the Lord, how he may please the Lord; but one who is married is concerned about the things of the world, how he may please his wife, and his interest is divided" (1 Cor. 7:32-34, NASB).

One of the reasons why Paul was able to travel so widely and devote so much time to the ministry was his gift of celibacy. It must also be recognized that celibacy should not be a requirement for ministry. Paul warns that forbidding believers to marry in later times comes from men who follow deceiving spirits (1 Tim. 4:1-5).

Motivations That Characterize the Gift of Celibacy

1. To remain single for the sake of the gospel.
2. To spend more time with the Lord in the devotional life.
3. To please the Lord with this gift of celibacy.
4. To have ministry where married workers would find it difficult.
5. To have a ministry with the "singles group."

Manifestations That Characterize the Gift of Celibacy

1. Can accept the single life without frustration.
2. Show the ability to put the work of Christ above personal

46

interests.

3. Have remained single to serve the Lord.
4. Give an unusual amount of time to ministry and devotions.
5. Indifferent to personal concerns and cares deeply for others.

Notes

1. Gangel, *Your Spiritual Gifts,* p. 36.
2. Kittel, *Theological Dictionary,* 3:1036.
3. Fuller Evangelistic Association, *Spiritual Gifts and Church Growth, Spiritual Gifts Leader's Guide* (Pasadena: Fuller Evangelistic Association, 1978), p. 18.
4. Wagner, *Your Spiritual Gifts,* p. 63.

6

Gifts of Word of Wisdom, Word of Knowledge, Faith, and Healings

The Gift of the Word of Wisdom

The gift of the word of wisdom is the Spirit-given ability to wisely apply the knowledge of God's Word in a given situation (1 Cor. 12:8).

In the opening chapters of Corinthians the wisdom of God is contrasted with the wisdom of the world. With all its wisdom the world failed to know God (1 Cor. 1:21), and believed the cross of Christ which is the wisdom of God to be foolishness (v. 23). The believer recognizes Christ as the expression of the wisdom of God (vv. 24, 30) and the Bible as the textbook of wisdom (2 Tim. 3:15).

While every believer is expected to act wisely and ask of God who gives to all men liberally (James 1:5), the believer with the gift of the word of wisdom arrives at solutions to complicated problems with spiritual insight which is beyond the ability of the average believer. The term wisdom is preceded by the phrase, "the word of" which suggests that the gift operates in a given situation when the Spirit reveals the solution for that moment. When the answer is given by the gifted saints, believers recognize immediately that this is the wisdom of God. When Solomon informed the women what should be done when the child was brought before him, the people "saw that the wisdom of God was in him" (1 Kings 3:28). In contrast to general wisdom, which is available to all believers, the gifted believer will consistently make wise decisions which will be pure, peaceable, gentle, reasonable, full of mercy and good fruits, unwavering, and without hypocrisy (James 3:17). Rick Yohn stresses that this gift operates in conjunction with the Word of God:

The gift of wisdom is biblically orientated. . .It

48

applies God's truth to contemporary problems. It never counsels a person to do anything contrary to God's will. Christian psychologists, marriage counselors, pastors and laymen who have this gift won't tell their counselees to take a course of action inconsistent with God's will.[1]

Motivations That Characterize the Gift of Wisdom

1. To provide insights from the Bible to problems that bother believers.
2. To study the Bible to find principles to apply to life.
3. To give words of wisdom for a specific problem in the church.
4. To give an answer to a heated debate that relieves tension.
5. To clarify a situation and formulate a satisfactory solution.

Manifestations That Characterize the Gift of Wisdom

1. Speak with such insight that others listen.
2. Have the ability to arrive at solutions to difficult problems.
3. Apply scriptural principles to life situations.
4. Seem to perceive a situation when others cannot.
5. Know how to find the correct biblical principle to cover a problem.

The Gift of the Word of Knowledge

The gift of the word of knowledge is the Spirit-given ability to analyze and systematize biblical truth along with the ability to recall particular segments of that truth when needed for a given situation (1 Cor. 12:8).

The term, "word of knowledge" then may be applied in two different ways. First, this gift is the ability to be a theologian, bringing the teachings of Scripture into a system or it may be on some occasions a situational communication. The Holy Spirit may instantaneously enlighten the gifted believer with the special insight needed by an individual or group. In either circumstance the end result of the ministry of this gift to the listener is understanding.

Evidently there exist three levels of knowledge:

1.   The natural man lives on the level of natural knowledge and is unable to comprehend spiritual truth (1 Cor. 2:14).

2.   The born again believer is on the level of spiritual knowledge and can perceive truth through the enlightenment of the Holy Spirit (1 Cor. 2:12, 13). Yet on this level the carnal do not clearly understand spiritual truths (1 Cor. 3:1-2).

3.   The believer with the gift of the word of knowledge is on a level of knowledge which is far above the level of the average believer.

Peter Wagner presents this insight into the word of knowledge:

> The person with this gift is a lead learner. He is expected to get the truth first and to originate new ideas. He is eager to learn, has a long attention span, and is able to absorb and retain unusual amounts of information. He is a scholar, at home with research, and is often found in the academic world. . . .[2]

In our day of increased humanistic knowledge, false philosophies, and experiential theology, the word of knowledge is essential to offset the inroads being made by these worldly systems. During this distressing time the gifted believer saturates his mind with the details of scriptural truth. His mind acting as a computer compares, analyzes, categorizes, and memorizes the great body of knowledge found in the Bible. He has a storehouse of scriptural knowledge. From this abundant resource, he is ready to reveal this knowledge at the right moment for a given situation or he is ready to teach it to the church.

The word of knowledge is often combined with other gifts resulting in a powerful ministry. When this gift is combined with teaching the gifted member makes a great contribution to the growth and welfare of the church. Bible schools, colleges, and seminaries are also enriched by the gift of the word of knowledge.

Jesus demonstrated this combination of gifts in His own ministry. The Sermon on the Mount draws from the whole of Scripture the essence of Christian conduct and ethics.

> *And it came to pass, when Jesus had ended these sayings, the people were astonished at his doctrine: For he taught them as one having authority, and not as the scribes* (Matt. 7:28, 29).

Motivations That Characterize the Gift of the Word of Knowledge

1. To analyze Bible truth.
2. To systematize Bible knowledge.
3. To memorize long segments of Bible passages.
4. To reveal Bible knowledge to believers at the right moment.
5. To study and interpret difficult passages of the Bible.

Manifestations That Characterize the Gift of the Word of Knowledge

1. Have the ability to discover the basic principles of biblical truth.
2. Are able to relate biblical truth in a system of doctrine.
3. Always give an in-depth treatment of a subject.
4. Are intellectually keen and thorough in scholarship.
5. Show ability to use Bible knowledge in ministering to the needs of other believers.

The Gift of Faith

The gift of faith is the Spirit-given ability to recognize what God wants to do in seemingly impossible situations and to trust God to get His work accomplished (1 Cor. 12:9).

This verse is not talking about saving faith which is necessary for the personal salvation of every believer. If a person does not exercise faith in Christ for salvation, that person continues to be lost. If the believer does not exercise faith in God's promises it is sin. But the gift of faith is a special faith given by the Holy Spirit that disregards insurmountable obstacles and claims answers to prayer.

Basically there are three types of supernatural faith: (1) saving faith (Eph. 2:8, 9); (2) faith which is the fruit of the Spirit (Gal. 5:22); and (3) the gift of faith which is a mountain moving faith which results in accomplishing humanly impossible tasks (Matt. 17:14-20).

Paul's ministry provides an illustration of the gift of faith and gives these basic characteristics of the gift as revealed in Acts 27:22-44:

1. He received a promise of what God wanted him to do (vv. 22-24).

2. He believed that God would bring it to pass (v. 25).

3. He maintained unswerving faith while in the hopeless circumstances (vv. 26-33).

4. He assured others that God would spare them (v. 34).

5. This assurance of his faith brought them cheer (v. 36).

6. His faith saved him and other prisoners from destruction (vv. 42, 43).

7. His faith spared everyone from death (v. 44).

George Mueller, who by faith operated an orphanage in Bristol, England, is the classical example of a modern believer who had the gift of faith. It is estimated that he cared for some ten thousand orphans over a period of sixty years. He received in answer to believing prayer $5 million to carry on this ministry. Through the gift of faith he was able to house two thousand orphans along with feeding them each day. One morning when no food was on hand, Mueller prayed, "Father, we thank Thee for the food Thou art going to give us." The next moment a knock was heard at the door. It was the baker who said, "I was awakened at 2:00 A.M. and felt I should bake some bread for you." A few minutes later a milkman arrived who said, "My milk wagon just broke down in front of your place. I must get rid of these cans of milk before I can take the wagon for repairs. Can you use this milk?" This was one of countless incidents in the life of George Mueller who possessed the gift of faith.

Motivations That Characterize the Gift of Faith

1. To believe that God will complete the work He has begun.
2. To have extraordinary faith despite contrary circumstances.
3. To have vision when others have no vision.
4. To believe God to supply needs in a supernatural way.
5. To rest in God's Word to perform the impossible.

Manifestations That Characterize the Gift of Faith

1. It is second nature to trust God to meet every need.
2. Have a clear idea of what God wants to do in a given situation.
3. Pray for specific needs so the answer can be verified.
4. Encourage other believers by the exercise of faith.
5. Show ability to exercise faith above that of most believers.

The Gifts of Healings

The gifts of healings is the Spirit-given ability to heal the sick and suffering believer (1 Cor. 12:28).

Most Bible scholars either interpret the double plural as referring to healing in the realm of the physical, emotional, and spiritual parts of the person or each healing in itself is believed to be a gift. Dr. A. B. Simpson explained the plural by saying, "These are various forms and ministries of healing."[3]

The greatest example of healing was Jesus who healed every kind of disease and every kind of sickness among the people. Matthew 4:24 states the following account of healing:

> *News about him spread all over Syria, and people brought to him all who were ill with various diseases, those suffering severe pain, the demon-possessed, the epileptics and the paralytics, and he healed them* (NIV).

The gifts of healings has been abused by many self-styled "healers" in our day who practice "faith healing." The claim is made that if a person is not healed, faith has not been exercised. A thorough study of this subject shows that this gift does not heal all of the time for Paul could not help Epaphroditus's illness (Phil. 2:25-27); Timothy's stomach condition (1 Tim. 5:23); and left Trophimus ill at Miletum (2 Tim. 4:20). Paul, himself, was not in good health (1 Cor. 2:3; 2 Cor. 11:30; 12:5, 7-10; Gal. 4:13), so Dr. Luke traveled with him.

Not all sickness is due to sin in the life of the afflicted as testified by Jesus who said, concerning the man born blind from birth, "that the works of God should be made manifest in him" (John 9:1-3). Yet God may withhold healing to discipline because of sin (1 Cor. 5:5; 2 Cor. 2:6-11) or for personal growth in humility (2 Cor. 12:7-9); or to add empathy to our character (2 Cor. 1:3, 4).

It appears that the normal use of the gift would be performed through the elders following the instructions given in James 5:14-16.

1.   The sick are to take the initiative and call for the elders (v. 14).

2.   The elders pray over the afflicted, anointing with oil in the name of the Lord (v. 14).

3.   The prayer of faith is based on the Word of God (Rom. 10:17) along with the witness of the Spirit to believe God for divine healing (v. 15).

4.   Confession of sin is essential for it is unlikely that one could exercise faith if he retains unconfessed sin in the life.

5.   The actual healing is by the power of God (v. 16).

Motivations That Characterize the Gifts of Healings

1.   To trust Christ for divine healing for the body.

2.   To fast and pray for divine healing in difficult cases.

3.   To practice divine healing according to James 5:14-16.

4.   To care for one's own body in a manner that glorifies Christ.

5.   To show the compassion of Christ for those who suffer physically.

Manifestations That Characterize the Gifts of Healings

1. Pray for others and healing occurs.
2. Through believing prayer have seen emotionally disturbed healed.
3. Serve as elder and through the "prayer of faith" have seen people healed.
4. In the name of the Lord physically sick people have been healed.
5. Show the ability to counsel the sick in preparation for anointing.

Notes

1. Rick Yohn, *Discover Your Spiritual Gift and Use It* (Wheaton: Tyndale House Publishers, 1975), p. 95.
2. Wagner, *Your Spiritual Gifts,* p. 218.
3. A. B. Simpson, *Christ In the Bible Series, First Corinthians* (Harrisburg: Christian Publications, Inc.), p. 94.

7

Gifts of Miracles, Discernment, Tongues and Interpretation of Tongues

The Gift of Miracles

The gift of miracles is the Spirit-given ability to believe God for mighty acts contrary to natural laws and that God receives the recognition for the miraculous event (1 Cor. 12:10, 28, 29).

The word miracle comes from the Greek word, *dunamis,* and is defined by Vine as "power, inherent ability, and is used of works of a supernatural origin and character, such as could not be produced by natural agents and means."[1] The Gospel is the power (*dunamis*) of God that produces salvation (Rom. 1:16). Every new birth experience is a miraculous event which is the evidence of the supernatural power of God. This is by far the greatest miracle which occurs with greater regularity than signs, wonders, and powers (2 Cor. 12:2) which are of secondary importance. These secondary events are sometimes necessary in the sovereignty of God to display His power so that people will listen to His message.

In the Old Testament Moses demonstrated his authority through the miracles of God so that the people would listen to God's message (Exod. 4:1-5). In the New Testament the miracles of Jesus recorded in John's Gospel demonstrated His deity resulting in people believing in Him and thereby receiving eternal life.

> *Jesus did many other miraculous signs in the presence of his disciples, which are not recorded in this book. But these are written that you may believe that Jesus is the Christ, the Son of God, and that by believing you may have life in his name* (John 20:30-32, NIV).

Rick Yohn makes the observation that "approximately 31 percent of the verses in Mark's Gospel alone deal with miracles."[2] This gift is closely associated with the gift of faith, and gifts of healings. All miracles are not from God. False christs and false prophets perform miracles and deceive many (Matt. 24:24).

Dr. A. B. Simpson answers the question of why we do not see miracles occur with more regularity by the following remarks:

> A miracle. . .is more bold and startling, involving a suspension of natural law and an effect so impressive as to become to all observers a distinct manifestation of the presence and power of God. These meteor flashes of supernatural power would lose their very emphasis if they were to become so frequent as to cease to be extraordinary.[3]

Motivations That Characterize the Gift of Miracles

1. To believe God for miracles.
2. To have power to heal instantaneously.
3. To have power over demons.
4. To see whole communities awakened and many saved.
5. To believe God for the miracle of new birth in difficult persons.

Manifestations That Characterize the Gift of Miracles

1. Experienced God's intervention in impossible situations.
2. The "prayer of faith" brought instantaneous healing.
3. People relate that your prayers have brought miracles of God.
4. Prayer has resulted in a miraculous change of events.
5. Unusual events keep occurring that reveal God's intervention.

The Gift of Discernment

The gift of discernment of spirits is the Spirit-given ability to discern whether information that claims to be of God is satanic, human, or divine (1 Cor. 12:10).

The word discernment comes from the Greek word, *diakrisis,* which means to judge or evaluate. The central idea is to have the faculty for distinguishing between truth and error. This gift is particularly associated with prophecy and the ability to discern whether a prophecy is of God or from a false prophet. It is clear from the New Testament that many false prophets have existed (1 John 4:1) and their number will increase before the return of Christ (Matt. 24:11). This is God's gift to the Church to protect it from error and falsehood.

But does not every believer have this gift? The Bible teaches that every believer who is mature is able to distinguish between good and evil (Heb. 5:12-14). As a believer grows in Christ (Eph. 4:14-15) spiritual discernment increases. But this gift rises above the mature believer's ability to discern between the spirit of truth and the spirit of error (1 John 4:1-3). The gifted believer is able to identify immediately whether the person giving the information is motivated by a wrong spirit.

Satan masquerades as an angel of light and the false apostles are masked as the apostles of Christ (2 Cor. 11:14, 15). The gifted believer has the Spirit-given ability to unmask Satan's disguise, to detect false teachers, and can spot phonies before others are aware of what is taking place.

Evidently Peter had this gift. When Ananias and Sapphira brought the money to the apostles from the sale of their property, Peter discerned a wrong spirit. He said, "Ananias, why hath Satan filled thine heart to lie to the Holy Ghost, and to keep back part of the price of the land?" (Acts 5:3). Later when Simon of Samaria tried to buy the power of the Holy Spirit, Peter told Simon to repent of this wickedness. He said, "For I perceive that thou art in the gall of bitterness, and in the bond of iniquity" (Acts 8:23).

Paul used the gift of discernment when a girl who possessed a spirit of divination followed him and his companions for several days. She cried out, "These men are the servants of the most high God, which shew unto us the way of salvation" (Acts 16:17). Paul discerned the statement as coming from a satanic spirit so he exorcised the spirit.

John's exhortation to "test the spirits" (1 John 4:1) is needed today with the rise of cults and the occult in our generation.

Motivations That Characterize the Gift of Discernment of Spirits

1. To expose error.
2. To reveal false prophecy.
3. To analyze what people say to detect half-truths.
4. To exorcise demons from possessed persons.
5. To protect the church from incorrect doctrine.

Manifestations That Characterize the Gift of Discernment of Spirits

1. Show the ability to perceive a phony when others are deceived.
2. Can identify immediately false prophecy.
3. Have keen insight into people's motives.
4. Can recognize whether a teaching is from Satan, God or human.
5. Ability to see errors that others miss in religious books.

The Gift of Tongues

The gift of tongues is the Spirit-given ability that enables a believer to receive and to speak a divine utterance in a language unknown to him (1 Cor. 12:10, 28).

Since tongues is one of many gifts sovereignly bestowed by the Holy Spirit, (1 Cor. 12:11), it is not a mark of spirituality nor is it a sign of the baptism of the Holy Spirit. Though they possessed all of the spiritual gifts, the Corinthians were rebuked as being carnal (1 Cor. 3:3). Dr. Simpson had this to say about tongues:

This gift seems to have been abused from an early period and turned rather to the display of spiritual pride than to the edification of the Church, and appears to have been withdrawn, in a great measure, at least, at an early day. Its apparent revival in modern times has been associated with much confusion, and created grave doubts respecting its preeminent value as compared, at least with other gifts of the Spirit.[4]

The Greek word for tongues is *glossa* which means language. Speaking in languages which are foreign to the believer is done totally in private unless interpreted. Paul makes it clear that he would rather speak five words with his understanding than ten thousand words spoken in tongues (1 Cor. 14:18-19). Notice the phrase "in church." Wayne Robinson makes this observation from a mathematical viewpoint:

It takes 10,000 words of tongues to equal five rationally spoken words—a ratio of 2,000 to 1. That's a rather devastating indictment of tongues when practiced in church. Yet, Paul still claims to be the greatest tongues speaker of all. One possible resolution is that Paul is redirecting the importance of tongues from the level of public display to the dimension of personal edification in private.[5]

The main value of tongues is that it is a form of prayer inspired by the Holy Spirit (1 Cor. 14:2) and the gifted person who speaks privately in a tongue edifies himself (1 Cor. 14:4). The public use is so prone to cause difficulties and misunderstandings that it must be regulated.

Tongues can be counterfeited and believers deceived, especially those who are taught that all believers must speak in tongues sooner or later to display spirituality. This false charismatic viewpoint has picked up momentum and reports of exposure of false tongues are increasing. K. Neill Foster gives the following report:

One brother who has tested tongues for forty years says that in his experience nine out of ten were false. In a recently published article one of our contemporaries cites a similar statistic: Ninety percent of the tongues he and his colleagues have tested have been false. In my own experience perhaps eighty percent of the tongues manifestations that I have had to deal with have been false.[6]

Motivations That Characterize the Gift of Speaking in Tongues

1. To worship and pray in tongues alone in private.
2. To receive the edification that comes from praying in tongues.
3. To speak in tongues in church when an interpreter is present.
4. To speak to God in a tongue which is foreign to you.
5. To pray with the Spirit and sing with the Spirit.

Manifestations That Characterize the Gift of Speaking in Tongues

1. Have spoken in tongues.
2. Pray in tongues when alone.
3. Have spoken in tongues in public only when interpreter is present.
4. Pray in tongues and are edified and Jesus is glorified.
5. The speaking in tongues is controlled and orderly.

The Gift of Interpretation

The gift of interpretation is the Spirit-given ability to interpret the message of a believer using the gift of tongues (1 Cor. 12:10).

The purpose of this gift is the edification of the church. If no interpreter is present, the tongues speaker must be confined to exercise this gift privately (1 Cor. 14:28). Tongues spoken in public must always be interpreted or it is useless and has no place in the church (vv. 27, 28). When interpreted it becomes a prophecy capable of edification, exhortation, and comfort (v. 3).

No matter how important the message that would be uttered, it would not be understood. Paul likens this uselessness to instruments of music (v. 7) which do not give distinct sounds. If a trumpet gave an uncertain sound, a soldier would not know whether or not to prepare for battle (v. 8). Likewise, speaking in tongues is useless unless it has a meaningful message (v. 9). Though there are many languages in the world, yet none are used for display, but to be understood (vv. 10, 11).

Since the believer ought to desire spiritual gifts, he ought to seek to excel in ways that will build up the church (v. 12). "For this reason the man who speaks in a tongue should pray that he may interpret what he says" (v. 13, NIV). While the gift of interpretation is different from the gift of tongues, one person may possess both gifts. A number of writers believe that the majority of Christians with one of these gifts possesses the other as well.

Since the gift of tongues is the most abused gift, it should be highly regulated when used in public. In one meeting, two or three messages in tongues are the maximum to be given (v. 27). They are to be given one at a time and then followed by an interpretation. If no interpreter is present the tongues speaker must be silent (v. 28). So the purpose of the interpreter is strictly one of a public nature to interpret the message for the edification of the body. Otherwise the gift of tongues would be useless in public.

Motivations That Characterize the Gift of Interpretation

1. To interpret tongues given in public.
2. To give the interpretation in an orderly manner.
3. To interpret tongues so the church will understand the message.
4. To interpret tongues so the body of Christ will be edified.
5. To interpret tongues so that Jesus will be glorified.

Manifestations That Characterize the Gift of Interpretation

1. Have interpreted messages given in tongues.
2. Show sensitivity by giving the interpretation in an orderly manner.
3. Have interpreted tongues which has edified, exhorted, and comforted the body.
4. Desire to glorify Jesus when giving tongues interpretation.
5. Pray for the interpretation when someone speaks in tongues.

Notes

1. W. E. Vine, *Expository Dictionary of New Testament Words* (Old Tappan: Fleming H. Revell, 1957), 3:75, p. 757.
2. Yohn, *Spiritual Gift and Use It*, p. 110.
3. Simpson, *First Corinthians,* p. 95.
4. Ibid., p. 96.
5. Wayne A. Robinson, *I Once Spoke In Tongues* (Wheaton: Tyndale House Publishers, 1973), p. 109.
6. K. Neill Foster, *Help! I Believe In Tongues* (Minneapolis: Bethany Fellowship, Inc., 1975), p. 89.

8

Gifts of Apostleship, Evangelism, Shepherding, and Hospitality

The Gift of Apostleship

The gift of apostleship is the Spirit-given ability to plant new churches and give leadership in the initial stages of development until a pastor can assume leadership (1 Cor. 12:28; Eph. 4:11).

The original twelve apostles were not the only apostles. They were the founding apostles and were distinguished from all other apostles in that they were actual witnesses of the Resurrection. After the Resurrection Jesus appeared to "the twelve" and then also to "all the apostles" (1 Cor. 15:5, 7). Men such as Paul (Rom. 1:1), Barnabas (Acts 14:14), Andronicus and Junias (Rom. 16:7), Apollos (1 Cor. 4:6, 9) and Silas (1 Thess. 2:6) were called apostles.

The word, "apostle," comes from a technical nautical term in the Greek language. It referred to an expedition with the admiral over a fleet of ships, who under the orders of his ruler, founded a colony. One chosen as an apostle would have great authority and would travel extensively either in surrounding or foreign lands. So in the New Testament the apostle was one commissioned as a messenger with authority to begin new churches. History reveals that new churches mushroomed wherever the apostles preached the gospel. Leslie Flynn notes the following:

> The word missionary is rooted in the Latin "to send," while the word apostle comes from the Greek "to send." Linguistically, missionary and apostle are equals. Both are sent ones. The missionary is sent from, as opposed to being called to a particular church.[1]

Paul was an outstanding example of this gift. He extended the church throughout the Mediterranean world. He would stay for a period of time, such as the three years spent at Ephesus (Acts 20:31), to give the church oversight in its beginning stages. When he had trained leadership, he left the church in their care and moved on to plant new churches.

Bobby Clinton presents the following insight:

> Traditionally the apostolic gift has been associated with missionary work since its pioneer-quality was immediately evident. However all who "go" as missionaries certainly don't have this gift and many who "stay" should recognize this gift and apply it to "pioneer situations" within their own locality.[2]

Motivations That Characterize the Gift of Apostleship

1.   To preach the gospel in unevangelized communities at home and overseas.
2.   To start new churches.
3.   To reach unreached persons with the gospel.
4.   To lay a doctrinal foundation for a new congregation.
5.   To move on to a new field when the church is established.

Manifestations That Characterize the Gift of Apostleship

1.   Helped begin and then led a new church.
2.   Have the ability to cross cultural and ethnic lines to minister.
3.   Unafraid to undertake what God wants done.
4.   Show the ability to face new situations with challenge and joy.
5.   Adapt easily to new environments.

The Gift of Evangelism

The gift of evangelism is the Spirit-given ability to persuade people to receive Christ as personal Savior and become His disciples (Eph. 4:11).

The word "evangelist," comes from a Greek word meaning, "one who announces good news." It appears only three times when (1) Philip is called an evangelist (Acts 21:8); (2) evangelists were given to the churches (Eph. 4:11); and (3) Timothy is commanded to "do the work of an evangelist" (2 Tim. 4:5).

The evangelist is primarily a messenger of "the good news." Philip illustrates a believer with the gift of evangelism:

1. He was willing to speak to people about Christ.

His message as an evangelist to the Samaritans was "the good news of the kingdom of God and the name of Jesus Christ" (Acts 8:12, NIV).

2. He was sensitive to the leading of the Holy Spirit and traveled wherever the Lord directed him (v. 26).

From preaching to the multitudes in Samaria he obeyed the Spirit and preached to one Ethiopian in Gaza (vv. 26, 27). Then he went to Azotus "and traveled about, preaching the gospel in all the towns until he reached Caesarea" (v. 40). So as an evangelist he traveled widely. There is no record of Philip engaging in a ministry wider than evangelism. Although he preached in an unevangelized area, he did not plant churches, but evidently left this work for the apostles to accomplish.

3. He used the Scripture to preach Christ to people.

When Philip preached to the Ethiopian he "opened his mouth, and beginning from this Scripture he preached Jesus to him" (v. 35, NASB). So Philip was experienced in both personal and mass evangelism.

4. The people responded by making a commitment to receive Christ (vv. 36, 37).

Philip had the Spirit-given ability to communicate the gospel. When people heard the message, many of them responded as the eunuch who received Christ and followed the Lord in baptism. The best evidence that one possesses the gift of evangelism is that people are coming to Christ in response to his ministry.

Motivations That Characterize the Gift of Evangelism

1. To proclaim Christ as personal Savior whenever possible.
2. To lead unbelievers to receive Christ as Savior and Lord.
3. To intercede in prayer much for the lost.
4. To follow up with discipleship training to conserve results.
5. To train new converts to lead others to Christ.

Manifestations That Characterize the Gift of Evangelism

1. Have personally led others to Christ.
2. Witness frequently on the job with some decisions.
3. Have the ability to turn conversation into a witnessing opportunity.
4. Able to move people with one's personal testimony of salvation.
5. Readily participate in the church's evangelism ministries.

The Gift of Shepherding

The gift of shepherding is the Spirit-given ability to care for, to protect from error, and to feed a group of believers with the Word of God (Eph. 4:11).

The word pastor comes from a Greek word that means, "shepherd"; hence the gift involves feeding, leading, guiding, caring, and protecting the sheep. The term pastor in Ephesians 4:11 is followed by the words, "and teachers." The word "and" has special significance in the Greek according to Walvoord who says the following:

> The use of *kai* linking pastor and teachers instead
> of the usual *de* implies that one cannot be a true
> pastor without being also a teacher.[3]

Without teaching, the pastor could not function properly. The pastor as a teacher has been called to equip the saints for the work of ministry (Eph. 4:12).

Although the word pastor is one of the preferred designations for ordained clergy, unordained laymen who are undershepherds in the congregation can have the gift of pastoring. This shepherding ministry can be performed by elders, Sunday school teachers, home Bible study teachers, youth sponsors, counselors, or deans in schools.

Timothy was an example of one who had the gift of shepherding. Paul addressed two epistles to Timothy that are called, "Pastoral Epistles." Here are instructions in 1 Timothy 4:11-16 that relate to a person with this gift:

1. Teach those doctrines that lead to godliness (v. 11).
2. Be an example and provide no opportunity for criticism (v. 12).
3. Read the Bible publicly for exhortation and teaching (v. 13).
4. Exercise and use your spiritual gifts (v. 14).
5. Concentrate on your ministry so progress can be seen (v. 15).
6. Carefully evaluate your gift of teaching (v. 16).

The Lord holds the believer with the gift of shepherding responsible for the care that he gives to a group of believers. The gifted person establishes a close and growing relationship over a long-term period so he can shepherd the sheep properly. Many churches have divided their congregations into cell groups of eight to twelve families and have assigned elders with the gift of shepherding to care for each of these groups. They meet together in homes sometime during the week for Bible study and to minister to one another's needs. Then they meet with the rest of the congregation on the Lord's day. The goal of the shepherd is to provide pastoral care that will develop his sheep toward maturity (Eph. 4:13).

Motivations That Characterize the Gift of Shepherding

1. To feed believers with the Word of God.
2. To guide believers by example in Christlikeness.
3. To perfect the believers to do the work of ministering.
4. To guard the body from being led astray by false doctrine.
5. To have an interest in the spiritual welfare of the body.

Manifestations That Characterize the Gift of Shepherding

1. Able to resolve problems between people.
2. Take seriously the responsibility for the spiritual welfare of a group.
3. Help to motivate the group toward a goal.
4. Know how to instruct and give spiritual guidance to a group over a long-term period.
5. Show a capacity to help believers with spiritual needs by prayer and the Bible.

The Gift of Hospitality

The gift of hospitality is the Spirit-given ability to cheerfully make a guest, whether known or unknown, to feel at home within your household (1 Pet. 4:9).

Hospitality comes from the combination of two Greek words which are *philos* meaning, "loving," and *xenos* meaning, "a stranger." The word hospitality has behind it the concept of loving concern for strangers. It is used as a noun in Romans 12:13, Hebrews 13:2, and as an adjective in 1 Timothy 3:2, Titus 1:8, and 1 Peter 4:9.

Peter exhorts to "Be hospitable to one another without complaint" (1 Pet. 4:9, NASB). This verse appears to flow into the next verse which says, "As each one has received a special gift [*charisma*] employ it in serving one another" (1 Pet. 4:10, NASB). So this close connection between hospitality of verse 9 and gifts of verse 10 strongly implies that hospitality is a spiritual gift.

The gift of hospitality is needed today as in the past. The early Christians followed the Roman roads to spread the gospel to the ends of the empire. This required travel under difficult circumstances. The believers opened their homes to provide lodging for the traveling evangelists. Hospitality helped to extend the gospel to the ends of the known world of that day.

When Jesus sent out the seventy workers He expected that they would be entertained in the homes where they ministered.

Leslie Flynn observed the following:

> Many traveling Christians carried letters of
> commendation. Not only did the traveler look to a
> Christian home for hospitality, but scattered
> believers looked to the traveler to bring word of
> Christ's work in other places, fostering a sense of
> unity throughout the world. Thus, hospitality was
> indispensable both to the entertained and the
> entertainer.[4]

Peter lodged "many days in Joppa with one Simon a tanner" (Acts 9:43) and he accepted an invitation to "tarry certain days" as a guest in the home of Cornelius (Acts 10:48). Paul was the guest of Lydia (Acts 16:15), the Philippian jailer (Acts 16:34), and on his last trip to Jerusalem in the home of Mnason (Acts 21:4, 7, 8, 16). Gaius received all the members of the church who crossed his threshold and permitted the church to worship at his house (Rom. 16:23).

The elder must have hospitality (1 Tim. 3:2). This will enable him to become better acquainted with fellow believers for greater ministry. Leaders who are hospitable toward strangers will set the example for the rest of the congregation to follow. If strangers feel at home, the church will have an opportunity for growth. There is one exception. False teachers are not to receive hospitality (2 John 10, 11).

Motivations That Characterize the Gift of Hospitality

1. To provide lodging for visiting speakers.
2. To wear out furniture if necessary to entertain guests.
3. To be surrounded by many persons rather than be alone.
4. To entertain without strain or frustration.
5. To make people feel "at home."

Manifestations That Characterize the Gift of Hospitality

1. Volunteer to provide food and lodging for visiting speakers.

2. Have ability to make strangers feel at home in my house.

3. Are willing to use home, sports equipment, and table setting for ministry.

4. Usually have a snack ready for guests soon after they arrive.

5. Enjoy entertaining believers from the church frequently.

Notes

1. Flynn, *19 Gifts of the Spirit,* p. 47.
2. Clinton, *Spiritual Gifts,* p. 64.
3. John F. Walvoord, *The Holy Spirit* (Grand Rapids: Zondervan Publishing House, 1978), p. 170.
4. Flynn, *19 Gifts of the Spirit,* p. 170.

Part Three

Testing to Determine Your Gifts

In Part Two you were asked to fill in the Evaluation Chart with your Discovery Group as each gift was given. Now that the final gift has been defined and evaluated, you should have some idea of what spiritual gifts you possess.

In chapter 9 all of the statements of motivation that characterize the spiritual gifts have been gathered from Part Two and compiled into a test to allow you to take another look at your inward desires and inclinations. This examination has been set up in such a way that the believer can evaluate in measurable terms the intensity of the motivation if it is present.

In chapter 10 all of the statements of manifestations that characterize the spiritual gifts have also been put together as in the test of chapter 9, but are measurable in terms of experience. Then to confirm gift discovery, the highest gifted scores of the motivational test are compared with the highest gift scores of the manifestation test along with the Evaluation Chart. These are evaluated by the believer and discussed with the Discovery Group along with the teacher.

This testing is based upon at least four considerations—
1. Consider your desires and inclinations.
2. Consider your experiences.
3. Consider your delights.
4. Consider the confirmation of others.

Kenneth Gangel gives the following helpful questions for gift testing:

> 1. What do you enjoy doing? God wants us to be happy in the service of the King. Christian ministry dare not become a neurotic compulsion to duty.
> 2. What has God been blessing? Do you see fruit from your teaching? Are people trusting Christ as a

result of your evangelism?

3. How have others encouraged you? God gives us parents and friends to help us in making key decisions like this.

4. What has the Holy Spirit told you? The inner witness of the Spirit is not limited to confirming our salvation. He wants us to know what our gifts are and how we are to use them.[1]

It is essential that prayer be offered by the leader for the guidance of the Holy Spirit on behalf of the believers before the testing begins. The student needs a prayerful attitude as the test is being taken. This is serious business and not a game to be played. There may also be a temptation to skip over the first two parts of this study and quickly take the tests without being knowledgeable about spiritual gifts. To get the most satisfying and accurate results, it is recommended to wait until you have gone through the process of this gift study along with the counsel of your gift Discovery Group and instructor. "In the multitude of counsellors there is safety" (Prov. 11:14b; 24:6b).

Some believers may question whether an evaluation of spiritual gifts is encouraged in the Scriptures. Romans 12:3 (NIV), tells us, "But rather think of yourself with sober judgment." In other words, "You should have a correct evaluation of yourself." This indicates that we should evaluate ourselves in the area of spiritual gifts. These tests are not conclusive, but can give strong indication of our spiritual gifts.

9

Test to Help Determine Your Gifts

Below are 100 statements which may help you find your spiritual gift or gifts. Please rate yourself with the following scale by writing the appropriate number at the right of the page.

Score your own reactions and desires with regard to each gift with the following scale:

Much	3
Some	2
Little	1
Not at all	0

After you have completed the test by rating yourself for each of the 100 statements, add the scores under each gift. Then take the five highest scored gifts and write on the lines provided at the end of the test.

Prophecy

1. To preach openly against sin.   2
2. To correct the wrongs of society.   2
3. To take a strong stand on contemporary issues.   3
4. To wake up an indifferent church.   0
5. To preach messages on future judgment along   0
   with Christ's return.

                                              Total   1

Helps

6. To do little jobs which will free leadership to   1
   use their gifts.

74

7. To do work myself rather than enlisting aid from others. _3_
8. To help people with short-term assignments. _1_
9. To be quiet rather than outspoken. _1_
10. To work with hands rather than speak before a group. _3_

Total _9_

Teaching

11. To analyze Bible knowledge. _3_
12. To systematize Bible knowledge. _2_
13. To research in order to prove Bible truths. _0_
14. To teach by truth and example so others will learn. _0_
15. To instruct others in discipleship and Christ-likeness. _0_

Total _5_

Exhortation

16. To encourage believers who are discouraged. _0_
17. To go out of the way to cheer people. _2_
18. To share Scriptures that will encourage others. _0_
19. To counsel believers with the Word. _0_
20. To search and find Scriptures that will help solve problems. _0_

Total _2_

Giving

21. To help others with money. _3_
22. To make money primarily to give for the spread of the gospel. _0_
23. To sacrifice all material goods if God required it. _1_
24. To share one's goods with the poor. _3_
25. To encourage others to give sacrificially. _1_

Total _8_

Administration

26. To assume responsibility when leadership is absent. _0_
27. To organize and motivate believers to do the Lord's work. _0_
28. To provide leadership to enable believers to reach goals. _0_
29. To lead a project to get work done with speed and effectiveness. _0_
30. To serve the Lord by leading others. _0_

Total _0_

Mercy

31. To alleviate the suffering of humanity. _3_
32. To remove emotional and physical pain from people. _3_
33. To visit the lonely and shut-ins. _2_
34. To minister to hopeless cases of humanity. _3_
35. To be kind and loving to the unwanted. _2_

Total _13_

Celibacy

36. To remain single for the sake of the gospel. _0_
37. To spend more time with the Lord in the devotional life. _____
38. To please the Lord with this gift of celibacy. _____
39. To have ministry where married workers would find it difficult. _____
40. To have a ministry with the "singles group." _____

Total _____

Word of Wisdom

41. To provide insights from the Bible to problems that bother believers. _1_

42. To study the Bible to find principles to apply to life. _2_

43. To give word of wisdom for a specific problem in the church. _0_

44. To give an answer to a heated debate that relieves tension. _0_

45. To clarify a situation and formulate a satisfactory solution. _0_

Total _3_

Word of Knowledge

46. To analyze Bible truth. _3_
47. To systematize Bible knowledge. _2_
48. To memorize long segments of Bible passages. _1_
49. To reveal Bible knowledge to believers at the right moment. _0_
50. To study and interpret difficult passages of the Bible. _1_

Total _7_

Faith

51. To believe that God will complete the work He has begun. _3_

52. To have extraordinary faith despite contrary circumstances. _3_

53. To have vision when others have no vision. _2_

54. To believe God to supply needs in supernatural ways for the body. _1_

55. To rest in God's Word to perform the impossible. _1_

Total _10_

Healings

56. To trust Christ for divine healing for own body. _2_
57. To fast and pray for divine healing for difficult cases. _0_

58. To practice divine healing according to James 5:14-16. _O_

59. To care for one's own body in a manner that glorifies Christ. _O_

60. To show the compassion of Christ for those who suffer physically. _2_

Total _4_

Miracles

61. To believe God for miracles. _2_
62. To have power to heal instantaneously. _O_
63. To have power over demons. _O_
64. To see whole communities awakened and many saved. _O_
65. To believe God for the miracle of new birth for difficult persons. _1_

Total _3_

Discerning of Spirits

66. To expose error. _O_
67. To reveal false prophecy. _O_
68. To analyze what people say to detect half-truths. _O_
69. To exorcise demons from possessed persons. _O_
70. To protect my church from incorrect doctrine. _O_

Total _O_

Tongues

71. To worship and pray in tongues when alone. _O_
72. To receive the edification that comes from praying in tongues. _O_
73. To speak in tongues in church when an interpreter is present. _O_
74. To speak to God in a tongue which is foreign to you. _O_

75. To pray with the Spirit and sing with the Spirit. _____0_____

Total _____6_____

Interpretation of Tongues

76. To interpret tongues given in public. _____0_____
77. To give interpretation in an orderly manner. _____0_____
78. To interpret tongues so the church will understand the message. _____0_____
79. To interpret tongues so the body of Christ will be edified. _____0_____
80. To interpret tongues that Jesus may be glorified. _____0_____

Total _____0_____

Apostleship

81. To preach the gospel at home and overseas in unevangelized communities. _____0_____
82. To start new churches. _____0_____
83. To reach unreached persons with the gospel. _____0_____
84. To lay a doctrinal foundation of a new congregation. _____0_____
85. To move on to a new field when the church is established. _____0_____

Total _____0_____

Evangelism

86. To proclaim Christ as personal Savior whenever possible. _____1_____
87. To lead unbelievers to receive Christ as Savior and Lord. _____2_____
88. To intercede in much prayer for the lost. _____3_____
89. To follow up with discipleship training to conserve results. _____2_____
90. To train new converts to lead others to Christ. _____2_____

Total _____10_____

Shepherding

91.	To feed believers with the Word of God.	2
92.	To guide believers by example in Christlikeness.	2
93.	To perfect the believers to do the work of ministering.	0
94.	To guard the body from being led astray by false doctrine.	0
95.	To have an interest in the spiritual welfare of the body.	2
	Total	6

Hospitality

96.	To provide lodging for visiting speakers.	0
97.	To wear out furniture if necessary to entertain guests.	2
98.	To be surrounded by many persons rather than be alone.	2
99.	To entertain without strain or frustration.	2
100.	To make people feel "at home."	2
	Total	8

Place the spiritual gifts with the highest scores on the lines below along with the scores for each gift.

1.	MERCY	13
2.	FAITH	10
3.	EVANGELIsm	10
4.	Helps	9
5.	GIVING / Hospitality	8

Notes

1. Gangel, *Your Spiritual Gifts,* p. 13.

10

Test to Help Confirm Your Gifts

Below are 100 statements which are based essentially on experiences manifested in your life. Please rate yourself with the following scale by writing the appropriate number at the right of the page.

This statement has been manifested in my life:

Much	3
Some	2
Little	1
Not at all	0

After you have completed the test by rating yourself for each of the 100 statements, add the scores under each gift. Then take the highest scored gifts and write on the lines provided at the end of this test.

Prophecy

1. Give timely messages that meet the needs of people. _0_
2. Able to correct persons who have made mistakes. _1_
3. Speak with such emotion that people are often moved to tears. _2_
4. Speak with authority when God gives a message. _1_
5. Believers receive edification, encouragement, and consolation from the message. _0_

Total _4_

Helps

6. Would rather assist a leader than be a leader. _3_

7. Enjoy doing manual and menial jobs around the church.   3

8. Generally are the first to volunteer for manual jobs at the church.   0

9. Do not find it difficult to help others.   3

10. Satisfied to be a teacher's aid in a Sunday school class.   2

Total   11

Teaching

11. Teaching in Sunday school has changed lives.   0

12. Explain truth in a clear manner so that people can understand it.   2

13. Usually research more material than can be used in one class period.   3

14. Spend time in word studies to assure accuracy.   0

15. The teaching ministry results in learning.   0

Total   5

Exhortation

16. A person to whom people readily confide their problems.   3

17. Advise people as to the right course of action.   0

18. Demonstrate a good grasp of the subtilities of human nature.   3

19. Able to guide people through the difficulties that produce maturity.   0

20. Give helpful insights to those going through hurts as well as joys.   0

Total   6

Giving

21. Do without in order to give more to further the gospel.   2

22. Donate funds when confronted with urgent financial needs. 2

23. Regularly give more than 30 percent of personal income to the Lord's work. 0

24. Show the ability to handle material resources wisely. 3

25. Can readily recognize the material needs of others. 1

Total 8

Administration

26. Can organize people and programs to accomplish goals. 0

27. Feel comfortable serving in a position of leadership. 3

28. Find it easy to make decisions and give directives. 1

29. Endure pressure until a goal is accomplished. 3

30. Are willing and able to delegate authority. 0

Total 7

Mercy

31. Enjoy helping people who have physical or mental problems. 2

32. Talk cheerfully to those who are lonely or shut-ins. 3

33. Discover that your visitation ministry cheers the suffering. 0

34. Attracted to people who are in distress. 3

35. Take food baskets to feed the poor. 3

Total 11

Celibacy

36. Can accept the single life without frustration. _____

37. Show the ability to put the work of Christ above _____ personal interests.
38. Have remained single to serve the Lord. _____
39. Give an unusual amount of time to ministry _____ and devotions.
40. Indifferent to personal concerns and cares _____ deeply for others.

Total _____

Word of Wisdom

41. Speak with such insight that others listen. _0_
42. Have the ability to arrive at solutions to _2_ difficult problems.
43. Apply scriptural principles to life situations. _1_
44. Seem to perceive a situation when others _3_ cannot.
45. Know how to find the correct biblical principle _0_ to cover a problem.

Total _6_

Word of Knowledge

46. Have the ability to discover the basic principles _2_ of biblical truth.
47. Are able to relate biblical truth in a system of _0_ doctrine.
48. Always give an in-depth treatment of a subject. _0_
49. Are intellectually keen and thorough in _2_ scholarship.
50. Show ability to use Bible knowledge in _0_ ministering to the needs of other believers.

Total _4_

Faith

51. It is second nature to trust God to meet every _1_ need.

52. Have a clear idea of what God wants to do in a given situation. _1_

53. Pray for specific needs so the answer can be verified. _3_

54. Encourage other believers by the exercise of faith. _2_

55. Show ability to exercise faith above that of most believers. _2_

Total _9_

Healings

56. Pray for others and healing occurs. _3_
57. Through believing prayer have seen emotionally disturbed healed. _0_
58. Serve as elder and through the "prayer of faith" have seen people healed. _0_
59. In the name of the Lord physically sick people have been healed. _0_
60. Show the ability to counsel the sick in preparation for anointing. _0_

Total _3_

Miracles

61. Experienced God's intervention in impossible situations. _0_

62. The "prayer of faith" brought instantaneous healing. _0_

63. People relate that your prayers have brought miracles of God. _0_

64. Prayer has resulted in a miraculous change of events. _0_

65. Unusual events keep occurring that reveal God's intervention. _2_

Total _2_

Discernment of Spirits

66. Show the ability to perceive a phony when others are deceived.   2
67. Can identify immediately false prophecy.   0
68. Have keen insight into people's motives.   3
69. Can recognize whether a teaching is from Satan, God or human.   1
70. Ability to see errors that others miss in religious books.   1

Total   6

Tongues

71. Have spoken in tongues.   0
72. Pray in tongues when alone.   0
73. Have spoken in tongues in public only when interpreter is present.   0
74. Pray in tongues and are edified and Jesus is glorified.   0
75. The speaking in tongues is controlled and orderly.   0

Total   0

Interpretation of Tongues

76. Have interpreted messages given in tongues.   0
77. Show sensitivity by giving the interpretation in an orderly manner.   ___
78. Have interpreted tongues which has edified, exhorted, and comforted the body.   ___
79. Desire to glorify Jesus when giving tongues interpretation.   ___
80. Pray for the interpretation when someone speaks in tongues.   ___

Total   0

Apostleship

81. Helped begin and then led a new church. _____
82. Have the ability to cross cultural and ethnic lines to minister. _____
83. Unafraid to undertake what God wants done. _____
84. Show the ability to face new situations with challenge and joy. _____
85. Adapt easily to new environments. _____

Total _0_

Evangelism

86. Have personally led others to Christ. _2_
87. Witness frequently on the job with some decisions. _1_
88. Have the ability to turn conversation into a witnessing opportunity. _1_
89. Able to move people with one's personal testimony of salvation. _1_
90. Readily participate in the church's evangelism ministries. _1_

Total _6_

Shepherding

91. Able to resolve problems between people. _0_
92. Take seriously the responsibility for the spiritual welfare of a group. _0_
93. Help to motivate the group toward a goal. _0_
94. Know how to instruct and give spiritual guidance to a group over a long-term period. _0_
95. Show a capacity to help believers with spiritual needs by prayer and the Bible. _0_

Total _0_

Hospitality

96. Volunteer to provide food and lodging for visiting speakers. — _0_
97. Have ability to make strangers feel at home in my house. — _2_
98. Are willing to use home, sports equipment, and table setting for ministry. — _2_
99. Usually have a snack ready for guests soon after they arrive. — _2_
100. Enjoy entertaining believers from the church frequently. — _2_

Total _0_

In column 1 place the gifts and the highest scores. In column 2 place the gifts with the highest scores from the last test. In column 3 list the gifts marked "yes" or "maybe" from the evaluation "confirm" column (p. 32).

Column 1	**Column 2**	**Column 3**
MERCY	MErcy	GIVING
HELPS	FAITH	ADMIN
FAITH	EVANGELISm	Mery
GIVING	HELPS	Faith
Hospitality	GIVING / Hosp	Evang / Hosp

After carefully comparing the above lists, place one or more spiritual gifts that you believe that God has imparted to you.

Faith   _Mercy_   _Celibay (pas_
Giving   _Evangelism_

Part Four

Developing and Using Your Gifts

The abilities inherent in the gifts of the Spirit can be enriched and improved by diligent development and faithful use of the gifts.

The development of a spiritual gift is a necessary step toward the use of that gift. Kenneth Gangel presents a clear illustration of his point:

> What would you think, for example, if your pastor indicated some day that he has the "gift of teaching" and, therefore, it will never be necessary for him to do any more preparation. From now on he will stand in the pulpit twice on Sunday and say whatever comes into his head because he is just "exercising his spiritual gift." Obviously, such glorification of ignorance is far from the New Testament intent.[1]

The failure to develop a gift may be a problem of attitude as suggested by Rick Yohn:

> A Christian may be gifted in music, but because he is lazy he refused to practice. Or he may feel if he just sings in church, voice lessons would be a waste of money. (In other words, anything is good enough for God.) Someone else may have a gift of administration. But he depends completely upon past experience. He never considers reading books on leadership or attending seminars that would help him develop his gift.[2]

Part Four suggests ways by which gifts may be developed and also proposes ministries by which they can be used of God. The mobilization of the gifts for the benefit of the local church is another issue addressed in Part Four.

Let it be understood that some of these suggestions may or may not prove useful. All of the suggestions presuppose that one is trusting the Holy Spirit for guidance in developing and using the gift. Those who use their gifts should check to see that they are always administered in love.

11

The Gifts Need to Be Developed

By development is meant the improvement of a gift by study and personal growth. The fact that a gift is supernatural in that it was given by the Holy Spirit does not negate the need for the recipient of that gift to develop its capability by ordinary study .and hard work.

How to Develop the Gift of Prophecy

1. Seek to build a good biblical background along with the ability to see God's plan as revealed throughout the Bible.
2. Study to acquire a working knowledge of the prophetic Scriptures.
3. Be aware of world news and how current trends affect the morality of the nation.
4. Discipline yourself to apply Bible truth to your own life.
5. Develop your communication skills by reading books on homiletics such as Broadus's *Preparation and Delivery of Sermons*, or James Braga's *How to Prepare Bible Messages*.

How to Develop the Gift of Teaching

1. Master hermeneutical principles based on the grammatical-historical approach to the Bible.
2. Have a program to master the Bible using an in-depth study of each book of the Bible along with a filing system for recall.
3. Apply all Bible truth you learn to your own life.
4. Study Jesus' teaching methods along with Gregory's *Laws of Teaching*. Study Larry Richard's books *Creative Bible Study, Creative Bible Teaching*, and *A Theology of Christian Education*.
5. Continually evaluate and improve your teaching methods and compare notes with other teachers for more effectiveness.

How to Develop Gifts of Wisdom and Knowledge

1.   Master Bible truths and especially those books of the Bible that are life related such as Proverbs, the parables, Romans 12-16, 1 Corinthians, Prison Epistles, Hebrews, James, 1 Peter, 2 Peter, 1 John, 2 John, 3 John, and Jude.
2.   Develop a devotional life along with the sense of God's abiding presence in the direction of your actions according to James 1:5, 6.
3.   Expect the Holy Spirit to call to your attention clear solutions to problems within small group discussions or to individuals.

How to Develop the Gift of Exhortation

1.   Study regularly those Scriptures which focus on the application of truth such as Proverbs, parables, Romans 12-16, 1 Corinthians, Prison Epistles, Hebrews, and James.
2.   Study Psalms, Job, and Ecclesiastes to help you become sensitive to people's needs.
3.   Read books by such authors as Jay Adams, Charles Solomon, and Gary Collins that use scriptural principles for counseling.
4.   Memorize verses which can be used to meet the needs of people in counseling.
5.   Be sensitive to the promptings of the Holy Spirit in which He will call to your attention experiences in the past that will help in present situations.

How to Develop the Gift of Discernment

1.   Master biblical truth by reading through the Bible regularly so you can recall its truths.
2.   Develop listening skills and the ability to question tactfully.
3.   Develop skills from books dealing with logical reasoning.
4.   Seek to exercise your gift.

How to Develop the Gift of Faith

1. Study Scripture such as Genesis 12-25, 37-50; Exodus 1-24; Deuteronomy 1-4, 7-12, 20, 28-32; Joshua, Judges, 1 and 2 Samuel; 1 and 2 Kings; Matthew-Acts; Romans 4; Hebrews 11; and note the special instances in which God intervened in the lives of His people.

2. Read books by F. B. Meyer on men like Abraham, Joseph, Moses, Elijah, Elisha, Samuel, and books about men with the gift of faith such as George Mueller and Hudson Taylor. Read books such as *Knowing God* by J. I. Packer, *The Knowledge of the Holy* by A. W. Tozer, and books on prayer.

3. Maintain a prayer notebook with specific requests and answers with dates in order to encourage your faith in God.

4. Pray together with a prayer partner who also has the gift of faith.

5. Seek situations to claim God's working and spearhead a prayer effort to trust God until you see results.

How to Develop the Gift of Giving

1. Study 2 Corinthians 8, 9; Philippians 4:10-19; 1 Timothy 6:3-10; James 5:1-6; Romans 12:8; Galatians 6:6; Ephesians 4:28b; 2 Corinthians 9:7, 8; James 2:2-4; and 1 John 3:17 to build principles and convictions to follow throughout life.

2. If you own a business, dedicate it to the Lord and expect unusual miracles in your business to enable you to increase your giving to further the gospel.

3. If you do not have great financial resources, you will still live comfortably with less than the average believer and direct your finances to worthy efforts.

4. Keep careful records of your financial transactions and study them. Pray for wisdom to use better methods of money management to enable larger giving.

5. Read books about believers possessing this gift such as Stanley Tam in his book, *God Owns My Business,* and R. G. LeTourneau's *Mover of Men and Mountains.*

How to Develop the Gift of Apostleship

1.   Develop a clear understanding of the nature of the Church through a study of the New Testament.
2.   Master, by in-depth studies, the pastoral and church epistles, selected leadership passages, and the Book of Acts.
3.   Make a special study of the biblical principles of missions. Read widely in missionary biographies and books on missionary methods.
4.   Develop skills in goal setting, planning, and evaluating along with a flexible attitude which can recognize the Spirit's confirmation on setting aside of certain plans.
5.   Study the revival movements, major movements in missions, church growth, church renewal, and reapply principles which can be used.
6.   If possible, train under a successful church planter.

How to Develop the Gift of Evangelism

1.   Study and memorize Scriptures that can be used to lead people to Christ.
2.   Study the approaches used by Jesus, Philip and other Bible examples of personal witness.
3.   Receive on-the-job training in your church by joining an evangelistic team, or going with a person that has developed this gift.
4.   Read such books as Coleman's *Master Plan of Evangelism,* Kennedy's *Evangelism Explosion,* and Leroy Eims's *The Lost Art of Disciple Making.*
5.   Take advantage of training programs that will teach you skills and methods in confronting people with the claims of Christ.

How to Develop the Gift of Shepherding

1.   Make a special study of leadership passages in order to use the Lord's leadership standards in your ministry (Matt. 18:15-20; 1 Cor.; 2 Cor.; Gal. 6:1-10; Phil.; Pastoral Epistles; Phile.; 1 Pet.

5:1-11). Memorize Proverbs 11:14, 22:3; Acts 20:28; 1 Thessalonians 5:12, 13; Galatians 6:1, 2; and Hebrews 13:7, 17.

2. Study the doctrine of the Church and be aware that God is working in the Church as a whole in terms of applied ecclesiology in our day.

3. Make a study of the spiritual qualifications of an elder and apply and model these standards in your life.

4. Study passages which will help you become sensitive to people's needs since shepherding involves caring for, and meeting needs of people (Prov., Ps., Job, Eccles.).

5. Study books on counseling such as Jay Adams's *Competent to Counsel, The Christian Counselor's Manual,* and *Shepherding God's Flock.*

6. Study the biographies of great Christian leaders.

How to Develop the Gift of Hospitality

1. Read Karen Mains's book *Open Heart Open House.*

2. Open your home for someone in your church to conduct a home Bible study.

3. Give the church secretary your name to provide overnight housing for visiting missionaries.

4. Have tracts, Christian books and magazines for guests to read. Gifts will not grow unless used and developed through an effort which is inspired by the Holy Spirit. It is not unspiritual to develop the gift through training or schooling to improve one's gift of teaching. Roy B. Zuck gives this perceptive insight in the area of development using the gift of teaching as an example:

> To develop one's teaching gift can in no way improve the quality or essence of what God has given. Development is simply for the purpose of enlarging the effectiveness of the gift. It is not a matter of adding good to that which is bad or only partially good, but rather adding growth to that which is implanted, development to that which is undeveloped, fruition to that which is latent.[3]

97

Notes

1.   Kenneth Gangel, *So You Want to Be a Leader* (Harrisburg: Christian Publications, Inc., 1973), p. 27.

2.   Yohn, *Spiritual Gift and Use It,* p. 145.

3.   Roy B. Zuck, *Spiritual Power In Your Teaching* (Chicago: Moody Press, 1972), p. 78.

12

The Gifts Need to Be Used

Who in church leadership has not had to fill a vacancy because of a moving member? Sometimes a growing church experiences the need of additional Sunday school teachers or elders. Then the question arises, "Who can fill these positions?" Under such pressure we can be guilty of placing personnel who are more willing than gifted to fill the vacancies. People are selected upon the basis of availability rather than their gifts. After a period of time the excitement wears off and the ministry becomes more of a burden than a joy, and an obligation more than a source of personal fulfillment. Soon numerical and spiritual growth begins to lag. In that circumstance the leader must be diplomatically removed from the responsibility. Then comes the nagging question, "Who is capable to replace the replacement?"

Dr. Tozer gives an apt illustration of pretending that his brain is trying to tell his ungifted hands to play the organ. He can only respond to his brain by refusing to even attempt to play the organ.

> You will agree that it would be foolish for me to try to bring forth any delightful and satisfying music using such ungifted members as my own hands.
>
> Is it not appalling then, to think that we allow this very thing to hapen in the Body of Christ? We enlist people and tell them to get busy doing God's work—failing to realize the necessity for the Spirit's anointing and control and functioning if a spiritual result is to be produced.[1]

It is anticipated that this study will help to eliminate this dilemma by placing members of the body in ministry according to their spiritual gifts. To begin this process, the members need to be knowledgeable in the subject of spiritual gifts and their place in ministry. Then a procedure is essential for the believers to develop their gifts and use them to fill places of responsibilities in the body. There can be no benefit realized from a believer's gifts if the leadership is not aware of his Spirit-given capabilities.

The three forms on the following pages are suggested as tools to guide church members in the discovery of the service the Holy Spirit has gifted them to give. It is essential to mobilize the body for a gift-centered ministry. The members of the church need to be placed in areas of service where their spiritual gifts will be utilized for maximum effectiveness and for the greatest possible blessing to the whole assembly.

The forms will also serve as a reference when the need arises to fill a vacancy. The first and second forms could be duplicated and given to the nominating committee as an invaluable aid in nominating believers to positions where their capabilities may be utilized.

The "Spiritual Gifts Profile" should be filled out when the believers have confirmation of their gifts. Then the "Personal Interview" form should be cared for as soon as possible. The "Job Description" should be filled out last. It is important to incorporate spiritual gifts in job descriptions for maximum ministry.

Spiritual Gifts Profile

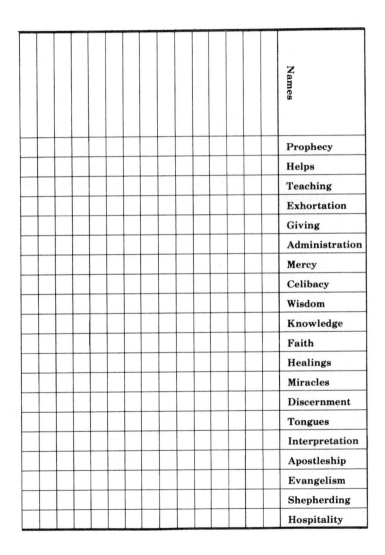

																		Names
																		Prophecy
																		Helps
																		Teaching
																		Exhortation
																		Giving
																		Administration
																		Mercy
																		Celibacy
																		Wisdom
																		Knowledge
																		Faith
																		Healings
																		Miracles
																		Discernment
																		Tongues
																		Interpretation
																		Apostleship
																		Evangelism
																		Shepherding
																		Hospitality

Personal Interview Form

Name _____ Age _____

Address _____ Phone _____

Member ( ) Yes ( ) No

Area of former ministry _____

_____

_____

Evaluate the above (for each area of ministry) in terms of your:
Personal enjoyment

1. _____

2. _____

3. _____

Successful Accomplishment and Peer Approval

1. _____

2. _____

3. _____

Of the above, the accomplishments I did best were:

_____

_____

In the light of your recent studies, what do you think are your gifts?

1. _____

2. _____

3. _____

4. _____

Where do you believe they can be best applied in the body?

_____

When will you be available for this ministry? _____

How long of a commitment are you able to make? _____

Other comments that would be helpful for your placement. __

_____

Job Description

Position _____

Job Description

Job Authority/Responsibility

Job Communication

    Reports to:
    Gets reports from:
    Works along with:

        Gifts required

_____

_____

_____

        Skills required

_____

_____

_____

Job Longevity: _____

Standard of Performance: _____

_____

_____

Comments: _____

_____

Notes

1. A. W. Tozer, *Tragedy in the Church: The Missing Gifts* (Harrisburg: Christian Publications, Inc., 1978), p. 38.
2. Fuller Evangelistic Association, *Spiritual Gifts and Church Growth, Part Three Workshop* (Pasadena: Fuller Evangelistic Assoc., 1978), p. 14.
3. Ibid., pp. 12, 13.
4. Ibid., p. 10.

The Church Needs to Function with Your Gifts

Believers may have discovered their gifts, developed them, and know where they can be used in ministry, but if a church is not structured for gift ministry, the gifts will not operate properly. What kind of structures within the local church will permit gifts to function according to the will of God? Three structural principles are essential for spiritual gifts to function properly in the local church.

The first structural principle to assure proper gift ministry is that the local church functions after the analogy of the body. It was shown in chapter 2 that God has organized the local church on the model of an organism (1 Cor. 12:12-27). One of the main features of the organism is that it shares life. It is the sharing of the common life that is vital to the health and welfare of the body. The sharing of spiritual life and gift ministry for the common good of the whole body is the very nature of body life. Believers must realize that gifts are not strictly for private use but for the benefit of the whole body. "But to each one is given the manifestation of the Spirit for the common good" (1 Cor. 12:7, NASB). All the members are dependent on each other. They care for one another and feel an equal interest in the health, harmony, and growth of the whole body.

Ray Stedman in his classic book, *Body Life,* describes this relationship that existed in the New Testament Church:

> What is terribly missing is the experience of "body life"; that warm fellowship of Christian with Christian which the New Testament calls *koinonia,* and which was an essential part of early Christianity. The New Testament lays heavy emphasis upon the need for Christians to know each other, closely and intimately enough to be able to bear one another's burdens, confess faults one to another, rebuke,

exhort, and admonish one another, minister to one another with the Word and through song and prayer.[1]

Each local church needs to cultivate this warm fellowship of the Spirit called *koinonia*. It is a matter of record that the renewal of New Testament *koinonia* has been widespread in the Church. Donald Bubna describes the movement in the following manner:

In recent years there has been much talk about a Holy Spirit movement in the church, and the word *koinonia* has sometimes been used to describe sharing of spiritual experiences. The Greek word implies something more practical than mystical. It simply says that through the Holy Spirit I have access to an intimate fellowship with God and with my Christian brothers and sisters.[2]

Besides experiencing shared life, the body experiences a shared ministry. Another characteristic of the renewal movement is the rise of the laity to share in the ministry which has been largely the domain of the pastor. David Haney made this observation:

Those at the headquarters and in the mainstream of the renewal movement are in unanimous agreement that the hope for renewal lies in the liberation of the laity. Call it what you will—the lay ministry, the universal ministry, the equipping ministry—it all means the same: that every believer is called to be a minister.[3]

This concept of ministry is a key factor in developing a healthy gift ministry in the local church.

Shared leadership must be added to shared life and ministry to complete the necessary congregational structure for gift ministry. Clyde Reid comments about shared leadership in the following way:

> The fruits of shared leadership are more theologically consistent with the goals and purposes of a religious fellowship than are the results when a highly authoritarian style is used.[4]

Reid presents this perceptive chart on the proportion of a leader's authority in relationship to a group's freedom:

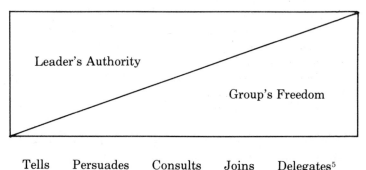

Tells   Persuades   Consults   Joins   Delegates[5]

A unique kind of spiritual leadership was introduced by Jesus in Matthew 20:25-28. He spoke of the Gentile rulers who rule over their subjects with great authority. Then Jesus said the following words:

> *Not so with you. Instead, whoever wants to become great among you must be your servant, and whoever wants to be first must be your slave—just as the Son of Man did not come to be served, but to serve, and to give his life a ransom for many* (NIV).

From these words of Jesus, two contrasting leadership styles emerge between the secular and the servant-leader as seen in the following chart:

	Secular	Servant-leader
1. Relationship:	"lords it over"	"among them"
2. Attitude:	Imposes his will	Gives himself for others' benefit
3. Power:	Uses it to impose his will	Inner power teaches followers to self-chosen commitment
4. Method:	Tells others what to do	Does and others follow through power of his example

Shared leadership is demonstrated in the local New Testament Church by a plurality of elders (Acts 20:28; 1 Pet. 5:1-3; 1 Tim. 5:17-19). However, in the first local church at Jerusalem, James arose to the position of leadership (Acts 15:13; 21:18; Gal. 1:19). No doubt this would be the equivalent of the leadership of the senior pastor and serves as a model for our present day church.

Dr. Keith Bailey tells how the pastor-elder and the lay-elder differ in vocation and in responsibility:

> The pastor-elder is a full-time minister of the gospel. He has abandoned secular labor to devote full time to the oversight and instruction of the church. The lay-elder is engaged in a secular vocation and ministers as an elder as time permits. . .The pastor is the constituted shepherd of the flock. He is to faithfully preach and teach the Word. He has oversight over all ministries of the local church.[6]

The structures of the local church should allow for shared life, shared ministry, and shared leadership through spiritual gifts. This kind of ministry will bring about the upbuilding of the body of Christ.

The second structural principle to assure proper gift ministry is that the local church be identified with the spirit of the cross. Jesus said, "Whosoever will come after me, let him deny himself, and take up his cross, and follow me" (Mark 8:34). There is a strong urge within the fleshly nature of the believer to be filled with pride in operating the gifts. The gift is misused when the flesh arises in a showy display. It always focuses attention on itself rather than on Christ. When self is on the cross and Christ is on the throne of a believer, the Holy Spirit always glorifies Jesus. The spiritual gifts are not given to call attention to the gifts but to Christ. When the cross is lost sight of, the gifts will not be used according to the will of God. Howard Snyder perceives this tendency to divorce spiritual gifts from the cross:

> It is the tendency on the one hand, to emphasize gifts in such a way that the cross is lost sight of and the community is fractured by self-centeredness, or, just the opposite, to deny any emphasis on gifts because of this tendency toward self-centeredness.[7]

It is clear that the Corinthians were not exercising their gifts in the light of the cross of Christ. For carnality, division, and pride were more evident than Christlikeness.

The third structural principle to assure proper gift ministry is that the local church bears the fruit of the Spirit. The gifts of the Spirit must be built upon the foundation of the fruit of the Spirit (Gal. 5:22, 23). Though all the spiritual gifts be in operation, yet if they are not motivated by love, they will produce nothing in the sight of God (1 Cor. 13:1-3).

After presenting the most complete instructions on the nature of love in the Bible in 1 Corinthians 13, chapter 14:1 gives the command to "Follow the way of love" (NIV). Placing this love chapter in the middle of the two gift chapters further demonstrates the essential need of the body to minister the gifts in the context of love. Rick Yohn describes love as being first on God's priority list:

> First on God's priority list is that the church

pursues love (I Cor. 14:1). **Jesus didn't say that "all men shall know that you are my disciples by your gifts."** He said, "By this all men will know that you are my disciples, if you have love for one another" (John 13:35). God judges a church's discipleship on the basis of the members' love for each other, not on the number or quality of their gifts. Many congregations pursue programs. Others pursue new members. Others pursue methods and organizations. The Bible tells us to pursue love.[8]

It is the Spirit-filled life that produces love. The Spirit-filled life motivates the believer to be like Jesus, produces holy living, and equips the believer for the proper use of gift ministry. This Spirit-filled life overflows like rivers of living water (John 7:38, 39) to touch the lives of others.

The local church needs a structure that will be conducive to love, ministry, and *koinonia*. It is only as this structure of love becomes a reality that a local body of believers becomes a fellowship prepared by God to bring forth beauty.

Notes

1. Ray C. Stedman, *Body Life* (Glendale: Gospel Light/Regal Books, 1972), p. 107.

2. Donald Bubna, *Building People* (Wheaton: Tyndale House Publishers, 1978), p. 41.

3. David Haney, *Renew My Church* (Grand Rapids: Zondervan Publishing House, 1974), p. 29.

4. Clyde Reid, *Groups Alive—Church Alive* (New York: Harper and Row, Publishers, 1969), p. 85.

5. Ibid., p. 82.

6. Bailey, *Servants In Charge,* p. 24.

7. Howard Snyder, *The Problems of Wine Skins* (Downers Grove: InterVarsity Press, 1975), p. 136.

8. Yohn, *Spiritual Gift and Use It,* p. 152.

9. Vine, *Expository Dictionary,* 3:75.

10. Howard Snyder, *The Community of the King* (Downers Grove: InterVarsity Press, 1977), p. 61.
11. Bailey, *Servants In Charge,* p. 14.

Conclusion

Paul reminded Timothy to "stir up the gift of God" (2 Tim. 1:6). The expression, "stir up," denotes "to kindle afresh, or keep in full flame."[9] It is a picture of a spark lying within the believer that needs to be fanned into a flame or it will surely smolder through neglect (1 Tim. 4:14).

It is anticipated that this study will be effective in fanning the hidden spark within many believers into a flame that will spread in the form of fervent ministry throughout the Christian community. Each believer can keep the full flame by faithfully using his spiritual gift as we see in the following verse:

Each one should use whatever gift he has received to serve others, faithfully administering God's grace in its various forms (1 Pet. 4:10, NIV).

The word "various" often expresses the idea of "many-colored" as in a rainbow or in a flower garden. Snyder said that "This suggests that the pure, intense but invisible light of God's glorious grace is made colorfully visible in the diversity of spiritual gifts in the Christian community."[10] When this transpires, Keith Bailey gives the exciting conclusion of what could happen in your church:

Activating the potential for ministry in their present membership could revolutionize many churches. Spirit-endowed workers could fill the many ministry needs of the church. When a believer learns to exercise his gift the work assignment becomes a blessed ministry rather than a drag. The success of evangelism, Christian education, the maturation of believers, discipleship, outreach, stewardship, ministry to the community, and prayer will depend on an adequate work force in the church.[11]

Notes

1. Ray C. Stedman, *Body Life* (Glendale: Gospel Light/Regal Books, 1972), p. 107.

2. Donald Bubna, *Building People* (Wheaton: Tyndale House Publishers, 1978), p. 41.

3. David Haney, *Renew My Church* (Grand Rapids: Zondervan Publishing House, 1974), p. 29.

4. Clyde Reid, *Groups Alive—Church Alive* (New York: Harper and Row, Publishers, 1969), p. 85.

5. Ibid., p. 82.

6. Bailey, *Servants In Charge*, p. 24.

7. Howard Snyder, *The Problems of Wine Skins* (Downers Grove: InterVarsity Press, 1975), p. 136.

8. Yohn, *Spiritual Gift and Use It*, p. 152.

9. Vine, *Expository Dictionary*, 3:75.

10. Howard Snyder, *The Community of the King* (Downers Grove: InterVarsity Press, 1977), p. 61.

11. Bailey, *Servants In Charge*, p. 14.

Bibliography

Allaby, Stanley R. "How To Discover and Test Whether You Have Teaching Gift." *The Journal of Pastoral Practice.* vol. 2. no. 2., 1978.

Bailey, Keith. *Servants In Charge.* Harrisburg: Christian Publications, Inc., 1979.

Bennett, Dennis, and Bennett, Rita. *The Holy Spirit and You.* Plainfield: Logos International, 1971.

Bittlinger, Andre. *Gifts and Ministries.* Grand Rapids: Wm. B. Eerdmans Publishing Co., 1973.

Bridge, D., and Phypers, D. *Spiritual Gifts and The Church.* Downers Grove: InterVarsity Press, 1973.

Christian and Missionary Alliance. *Seek Not—Forbid Not.* Nyack: C&MA leaflet.

Clinton, Bobby. *Spiritual Gifts.* Coral Gables: West Indies Mission, 1975.

Flynn, Leslie B. *19 Gifts of the Spirit.* Wheaton: Victor Books/Scripture Press, 1974.

Foster, K. Neill. *Help! I Believe in Tongues.* Minneapolis: Bethany Fellowship, Inc., 1975.

Fuller Evangelistic Association. *Spiritual Gifts and Church Growth. Spiritual Gifts Leader's Guide.* Pasadena: Fuller Evangelistic Association, 1978.

_____ . *Spiritual Gifts and Church Growth. Part Two Workshop.* Pasadena: Fuller Evangelistic Association, 1978.

_____ . *Spiritual Gifts and Church Growth. Part Three.* Pasadena: Fuller Evangelistic Association, 1978.

Gangel, Kenneth. *So You Want to Be a Leader!* Harrisburg: Christian Publications, Inc., 1973.

_____ . *You and Your Spiritual Gifts.* Chicago: Moody Press, 1975.

Getz, Gene. *The Measure of a Church.* Glendale: Gospel Light/Regal Books, 1977.

Gillquist, Peter E. *Let's Quit Fighting about the Holy Spirit.* Grand Rapids: Zondervan Publishing House, 1974.

Girard, Robert O. *Brethren, Hang Loose.* Grand Rapids: Zondervan Publishing House, 1972.

Gothard, Bill. *Discovering Your Spiritual Gift. Part 2.* Oak Brook: Institute in Basic Youth Conflicts, 1973.

Grossman, Siegried. *The Gifts of the Spirit.* Wheaton: Key Publishers, 1971.

Haney, David. *Renew My Church*. Grand Rapids: Zondervan Publishing House, 1974.

Howard, David. *By the Power of the Holy Spirit*. Downers Grove: Inter-Varsity Press, 1975.

Kittel, Gerhard. *Theological Dictionary of the New Testament*. Grand Rapids: Wm. B. Eerdmans Publishing Co., 1972.

LeTourneau, R. G. *Mover of Men and Mountains*. Chicago: Moody Press, 1972.

Lindsey, Hal. *Satan Is Alive and Well on Planet Earth*. Grand Rapids: Zondervan Publishing House, 1972.

Mains, Karen B. *Open Heart Open Home*. Elgin: David C. Cook Publishing Co., 1976.

McMinn, Gordon N. *Spiritual Gifts Inventory*. Portland: Western Baptist Press, 1978.

Reid, Clyde. *Group Alive—Church Alive*. New York: Harper & Row, Publishers, 1969.

Richardson, Stanton W. *Studies in Biblical Theology*. vol. III. St. Paul: St. Paul Bible College, 1969.

Robinson, Wayne A. *I Once Spoke in Tongues*. Wheaton: Tyndale House Publishers, 1975.

Sanders, J. Oswald. *The Holy Spirit and His Gifts*. Grand Rapids: Zondervan Publishing House, 1973.

Simpson, A. B. *Christ In the Bible Series, First Corinthians*. Harrisburg: Christian Publications, Inc.

_____ . *The Gospel of Healing*. Harrisburg: Christian Publications, Inc., 1915.

_____ . *The Holy Spirit*. vol. 2. Harrisburg: Christian Publications, Inc.

Smith, Bob. *When All Else Fails, Read the Directions*. Waco: Word, Inc., 1974.

Snyder, Howard A. *The Community of the King*. Downers Grove: Inter-Varsity Press, 1977.

_____ . *The Problem of Wine Skins*. Downers Grove: InterVarsity, 1978.

Stanger, F. B. *The Gifts of the Spirit*. Harrisburg: Christian Publications, Inc., 1974.

Stedman, Ray C. *Body Life*. Glendale: Gospel Light/Regal Books, 1972.

Stoesz, Samuel. *Understanding My Church*. Harrisburg: Christian Publications, Inc., 1968.

Thayer, Joseph H. *Greek-English Lexicon of the New Testament*. New York: American Book Co., 1889.

Tozer, A. W. *The Tozer Pulpit*. vol. 2. Harrisburg: Christian Publications, Inc., 1968.

_____ . *Tragedy in the Church: The Missing Gifts*. Harrisburg: Christian Publications, Inc., 1978.

Turner, Harry L. *The Voice of the Spirit.* Harrisburg, Christian Publications, Inc.

Vine, W. E. *Expository Dictionary of New Testament Words.* Old Tappan: Fleming H. Revell, 1957.

Wagner, C. Peter. *Your Spiritual Gifts Can Help Your Church Grow.* 2nd ed. Glendale: Gospel Light/Regal Books, 1980.

Walvoord, John F. *The Holy Spirit.* Grand Rapids: Zondervan Publishing House, 1978.

Woodcock, Eldon. "The Source and Purpose of the Gifts." *The Alliance Witness.* Oct. 18, 1978.

Yohn, Rick. *Discover Your Spiritual Gift and Use It.* Wheaton: Tyndale House Publishers, 1975.

Zuck, Roy B. *Spiritual Power in Your Teaching.* Chicago: Moody Press, 1972.